DRIVEN TO SUCCEED

STEVE D. ANDERSON

Driven to Succeed

Copyright © 2021 Steve Anderson

Printed in Canada

First Printing, 2021

Book cover photography: Althea Alli, ACCE Photography

Editing by: Kerri-Ann Haye-Donawa

ISBN: 978-1-9991698-2-4

ACKNOWLEDGEMENTS

Writing this book with the emotional backdrop of a global pandemic would have never been possible without the encouragement and support of my friends, family, and other supporters who cheered me on every step of the way.

Special thanks to Abid Mirza for working with me, encouraging me, and tolerating me on this journey that we undertook together. Your guidance and push for authenticity forced me to revisit memories and events I had long buried, and for that, I sincerely thank you.

I also want to shout out Kern Carter for his insight and encouragement.

DEDICATION

To my two "all-stars," Asia and Devante, who inspire me to be better each day and remind me not to take life too seriously. Both of you are working hard to achieve your dreams, and, as a family, we are proud.

To my angel on Earth, my mother, Carmen Anderson, who sacrificed and instilled hope when life seemed hopeless. Thank you for your continued prayers and your reminder that I should leave a legacy of excellence.

To the Shelburne community—thank you for trusting me to lead as your Deputy Mayor, and for allowing me to fulfil a dream that, as a youth, never seemed possible.

To the Jane and Finch community and all the hardworking families who do not get the recognition they deserve.

To God, whose words remind me that all things are possible if we continue to put our trust in Him.

Lastly, to everyone who has ever had a dream and questioned whether it could come to fruition because of current circumstances. I am here to tell you to keep pushing through, as there is light at the end of the tunnel.

Contents

Endorsements

"Steve Anderson's story exemplifies the importance of tenacity and focus in determining one's destiny. I am impressed and inspired by his resolve to reach his goals, regardless of the obstacles along the way. Instead of being hobbled by stereotypes, readers will learn that the only real limits are self-imposed. Now, more than ever, the disenfranchised, oppressed, and overlooked must rise to their full potential, regardless of circumstance. Steve's story continues the long cultural narrative of overcoming adversity to ascend the heights of achievement through academic and personal excellence. Read it and be inspired to emulate his experience."

Maurice
Medical Doctor, Canadian Armed Forces

"Steve Anderson's story is one of hope and inspiration. It epitomizes the power of determination and perseverance to overcome barriers and achieve one's true potential. Despite the obstacles placed in his path from a young age, Steve was able to defy the odds and become a positive influence in our society. Rising to great heights as the first black lawyer with the Toronto Transit Commission and Deputy Mayor for the Town of Shelburne, he has remained humble, always acknowledging his roots. Steve's story provides a rich resource for motivating our youths to aspire and work towards excellence, never allowing circumstances to dictate their destination. We are fortunate to have Steve as a role model, challenging and empowering our youth. His impact is phenomenal!"

Janetta Jarrett
Teacher, Toronto District School Board

"In an era where excuses, poor self-image, self-blame, and self-sabotage have become the reality for many youths, *Driven to Succeed* is the answer to shifting our thinking from a state of complacency to one of productivity, and from a state of negativity to one of positivity.

I have known Steve for over twenty years, and his achievements, character, and credibility speak for themselves. Both Steve and I grew up in the stereotypical "Jane & Finch" area, and the outcomes of our experiences, setbacks, and successes were not accidental but due to our commitment to self and our resilience to succeed, despite the odds. This book is proof that success has less to do with where you start, and more to do with how you decide to finish. The message of *Driven to Succeed* is simple: We all started somewhere, but everyone must decide to "FINISH HOW YOU WANT TO BE REMEMBERED."

Andrew E. Guy
Ted X speaker, Author & Branding Expert

———————————

Driven to Succeed is a thoughtful and inspirational account of a non-traditional pathway to success. Steve Anderson takes the reader on an autobiographical journey in his shoes and provides personal insight into a path less travelled. I've personally known Steve for over thirty years, having grown up in the "Jane and Finch" community myself. I have travelled on a similar path and am further inspired by Steve's words. The totality of Steve's experiences has led to a unique and diverse perspective, which has become the foundation for a model of success from a non-traditional background."

Driven to Succeed is a must read!

Ian Daley
Lawyer, Toronto ON

"Finally, a book that speaks about the black experience in Canadian politics. Steve has always been a champion for equity for those in his community. Steve draws from his various roles in the community to demonstrate that giving up should never be an option. We need to learn to use obstacles as motivation to be creative and move forward to achieve our goals."

Velma Morgan
Chair, OBVC

"I've known Steve Anderson for ten years, as he presented scholarship awards to exceptional Grade 5 graduates at Shoreham Public Sports & Wellness Academy, an elementary school in the Jane-Finch community. When Steve shared his story of growing up in the same neighbourhood and facing similar challenges with the graduates, their parents, and school staff, everyone in the auditorium listened. His message of hope links the importance of life choices and hard work, which resonated with children and families in the neighbourhood, as well as with school staff dedicated to enabling children to find and actualize their potential. Steve has shared his experiences with students at Brookview and Oakdale Park Middle Schools and the Jane-Finch Hockey Education Reaching Out Society (HEROS) youth mentoring program."

Tony Wray
Speech-Language Pathologist

"Steve is a strong, disciplined, and charismatic leader who speaks truth and leads by example. He is a true role model."

Jennifer Pereira
President of the Ontario College of Kinesiologist

INTRODUCTION

Success and financial independence are things we all strive to achieve, yet they allude many of us. The images of success frequently seen on social media, in music videos, and in blockbuster Hollywood movies often depict individuals who live in the best neighbourhoods, wear the most expensive clothing, and drive the fanciest cars.

When one, or even worse all, of these items do not resemble your current reality, you are often left feeling unworthy, embarrassed, useless, and doomed for a life of invisibility. At best, you can expect a life of mediocrity.

Growing up in the infamous Jane and Finch community, my life was far from the images of societal success. In fact, in the eyes of many, I was predestined for failure just by living there. I was a young, Black male from a single-parent household, living in a socioeconomically disadvantaged community. Using a baseball analogy, I had already struck out in life before my thirteenth birthday. If you were betting against me, you would have likely wagered everything on my journey ending up on the front page of the Toronto Sun Newspaper: Another racialized youth from the hood arrested or killed due to gang violence. After all, what good can come out of Jane and Finch?

The answer is plenty!

Just because you are written off by societal standards does not mean you must live a life defined by the expectations of others. When the world makes you feel like a depreciating asset, remember your history and understand that you are of significant value. Your unique circumstances and journey in life are by no means a failure because they do not resemble the popular path travelled by the majority. Continue to be self-assured and believe that success is attainable. For many of us, we will have to climb the rough side of the mountain to get to the top.

This book is a reminder that it is not how you start but how you decide to finish. Despite the appearance of insurmountable obstacles, if you continue to dream big, take decisive action, and have an unwavering drive to succeed, nothing, and no one, will ever hold you back. While the taste of success is personally gratifying, the hard truth is that it often comes at a cost. My journey also highlights the personal struggles that I, and many other racialized individuals, face even after achieving at the highest levels.

I invite you to join me as I take you on an authentic and emotional ride of setbacks, disappointments, and personal accomplishments. Buckle up and be inspired!

Chapter 1

Finding Myself in a Crowd

"The greatest challenge in life is discovering who you are. The second greatest is being happy with what you find."
– Amit

W HO AM I, and where do I belong in the grand scheme of life? Can I be myself? Will I be accepted? When we find ourselves seeking the approval and validation of others, it is worth asking these important questions. Does the decision to conceal our authentic self—value system, cultural heritage, and upbringing—get us any farther ahead in the eyes of those we are seeking to please? The very thing we are attempting to hide is what makes us unique, special, and separate from the crowd. Is it worth the aggravation attempting to become someone we are not?

For youths struggling to understand their own identity, how the above questions are answered, and the subsequent actions taken, can have life-altering effects. The outcomes are often social isolation and low self-esteem. Along my journey, I learned the hard lesson that I was not immune to these challenges.

From a young age, my own journey of self-discovery and acceptance was a wrestling match between the person I was and the individual I wanted to be. I struggled to find my place as the youngest in a large family. I was desperate to assimilate into the culture, experiences, and memories of a land that was foreign to me. It would take a while, but I would later learn that embracing my own identity and differences made me unique—and that was a good thing.

A Canadian in a Jamaican-born Family

My family's roots began in the proud and beloved country of Jamaica. Despite the promises of paradise and fantasies being fulfilled for revellers from around the world, there was nothing magical for many families who struggled to make ends meet. Finding it difficult to financially provide, my mother, after consulting with my father, made the difficult decision to leave her country of birth and her children behind to pursue a better life in Canada in the early '70s. Once established, my mother hired a lawyer and successfully petitioned Canadian Immigration officials to have the rest of the family join her a year later.

With the family reunited, my parents got settled in their first apartment in downtown Toronto. They earned a living initially with my mother working as a nanny and my father selling Avon products door to door. Only a few years in their new homeland, they got a welcomed addition to the family: me, Steve. I opened my eyes as a healthy baby boy, born weighing 6 lbs, 5 oz, at the Wellesley Hospital. Eventually, I was taken home and formally introduced to my large family, consisting of six brothers and one sister. My siblings—Clive, Lenna, Lenny, Hopeton, Linton, Wilton, and Chester—all had names that were commonly used in the island of Jamaica, except for me, the youngest child who had a name that stood out like a sore thumb.

Given my birth in a downtown Toronto hospital, and having received a typical Canadian first name by my parents, I was immediately set apart from the rest of my family. Thinking back, it did not take long for me to be consciously aware of my differences. The last name I shared with my siblings suggested that I was like everyone else, but it was not enough to patch the gap that I felt existed.

Over the years, I remember my childhood being normal and loving. Being the youngest in the family had its privileges and disadvantages. I was used to receiving special attention from my parents, but I would often get ribbed by my siblings. I was the adopted brother from another country. At dinnertime, my siblings would jokingly remind me of my place of birth whenever I opted for typical Canadian delights like pizza, fries, and hamburgers, instead of the popular Jamaican cuisine—rice and peas, curry goat, and oxtail. The teasing was good natured, as we all laughed about my stark food preferences. Although innocent, it was just another reminder that I was unlike the rest of my family. I left each experience wanting to be more like them. At that stage of my life, I did not see the value of standing out from the crowd.

By no means was I ashamed of my Canadian identity, but like most young people, I wanted to be a part of a cool group. It was difficult to put my finger on it, but there was something the rest of my family had by being born and raised in Jamaica that I didn't, and I wanted it. Upon reflection, a strong part of me wanted to be a true Jamaican "Yardie" (a person of Jamaican origin). At the time, I was so desperate to cultivate the identity and lived cultural experiences of my family that I strived for their identity at the expense of cultivating my own. The growing isolation I felt was usually amplified during major cultural celebrations hosted at our home. Extended family and friends would come to visit, and my mom would be in the kitchen all day cooking up a storm, making her best Jamaican jerk chicken, ackee and saltfish, yams, and my favourite golden fried plantains. Everyone would gather around the dinner table to enjoy foods from back home and share the stresses and struggles of being immigrants in a country that was far different from their own.

As the night went on, the formalities in perfect English would inevitably disappear, being replaced by the language of choice: Jamaican patois. For those unfamiliar with patois, it is defined as an English-based creole language with West African influences spoken primarily in Jamaica and among the Jamaican diasporas.

Inevitably, the focus would turn to life in Jamaica. I would listen wide-eyed at the dinner table as family members reflected fondly on stories of food, past relationships, and friends. My mother would always start the conversation recounting how many miles she would walk with the neighbourhood kids to get to school. She smiled the most when speaking about her favourite dog, Brownie. Her loyal companion followed her everywhere, and even waited for her patiently as she attended church service every Saturday morning. I often wished I could turn back the hands of time to see the dog that loved her unconditionally. It would have given me the opportunity to say "thank you." My mother was born and raised in an area called Chateau. She often shared her wild and entertaining adventures going to the market in May Pen with her donkey. No matter how many times she told this part of her story, it always elicited eye-watering laughter. Although funny, I found her stories of walking to the market with her donkey difficult to imagine, as I was accustomed to seeing people take public transit to get where they needed to go. Once my mother finished, my siblings would follow suit, eagerly chiming in with entertaining experiences of their own. As my family recounted their stories one by one, I was forced to use my imagination to visualize the settings, as I had yet to visit the island of Jamaica at the time. In many respects, I was off on my own island with nothing to contribute other than laughter and nodding when appropriate.

The feeling and the questions were the same after each event. What could I do to truly be a part of my family? I tried everything within reason to feel more connected. For weeks, I learned and practiced a few things in the privacy of my bedroom. Not brave enough to reveal what

I was practicing at major family events, I decided to test the waters first with my immediate family. One evening at dinner, I decided to unleash my rehearsed Jamaican patois in the hope of receiving acceptance and validation. Despite hearing the language spoken at home routinely, my efforts were nothing short of a disaster, since I was not authentic.

I was clearly the entertainment that evening, as the dining room erupted with laughter. It would be my first and last attempt. Shifting to my plan B, I tried listening to Jamaican music and attempted to copy the latest reggae dance move. I later abandoned that experiment after being given the nickname "Two-left-foot Steve." While my family indulged me with their time and attention, it was clear that I was not getting the acceptance I desired. I became more desperate with each failed attempt. It was obvious to everyone, except me, that I was trying too hard to act and behave as someone I was not.

As I began to plot my next move, a sudden change of events put that on hold. I finally got the opportunity to visit the country that I had explored only in my imagination. Unfortunately, it was the passing of my grandmother that eventually got me and my family to travel to Jamaica. I had mixed emotions about the trip. I felt excited and guilty at the same time. After all, I was attending a funeral and not going on vacation. In a matter of days, I was on my way to visit a place and person I had never seen or met before. I had heard stories of my grandmother and seen pictures, but that was it. It was hard to feel a connection to someone I did not really know. My feelings of sadness were more so for my mother and her loss.

When the plane landed in Jamaica and I officially stepped foot on the island, I acted like any other tourist taking in the Caribbean vibe and beauty. For the rest of my family, they were at home, and it showed in their countenance, attitude, and the way they spoke. It was obvious that they were all very comfortable being themselves without the fear of judgment.

Before the funeral, I had the opportunity to visit many of the areas I had heard of in family stories. As the days went by, I met a lot of people who had known my grandmother well. It was meaningful to hear people speak fondly about her and what she meant to their lives. Once again, I could not help but feel disconnected. They were speaking about a person that they assumed I knew well. For me, the conversations were somewhat awkward, as I would often leave these encounters not knowing what to think or how to feel.

The funeral came and went. Although I enjoyed the new surroundings, it was now time to return to familiar territory. My trip to Jamaica helped me to understand why this foreign country was so meaningful to my family. To my disappointment, it did nothing to eradicate my feeling of being an outsider among them.

The differences in my lived experiences compared to my family's made me realize that perhaps I would never fit in. It appeared I was destined to remain at odds with them for the rest of my life. For years, I focused on being like the people around me to no avail. Now at a crossroads, an unexpected move to a new community would give me all the clarity I needed. It was now time to focus my attention inwards.

Lost and Found: A New Beginning in Jane and Finch

Although my early experiences had an impact on how I viewed myself, my real journey towards self-discovery, which shaped my future path, began when we moved from downtown Toronto to Jane and Finch. I spent the first ten years of my life living in the heart of Toronto, and while this time was pivotal, it paled in comparison to the experiences that awaited me.

Not knowing anything at all about my new community, I was shocked by what I later discovered. For many, the mere mention of Jane and Finch immediately triggered an image reminiscent of a

Figure 1.1: Sitting with Ronald McDonald two weeks before my move to Jane and Finch

scary movie. The spotlight on the community was intense. Media outlets were largely determined to give prime coverage to the gangs, guns, and street crime. Little attention was given to those striving to make a positive difference.

Regardless of one's stance on the community, it was hard to witness, firsthand, the implications of widespread neglect by government officials who failed to invest and implement measures to lift the people out of poverty. Compared to the wealthier neighbourhoods, the socioeconomic disparities in Jane and Finch made it extremely difficult for some families to provide for their basic needs. Sadly, it was not uncommon to see children coming to school without a coat in the winter. The only protection from the harsh Canadian weather was a long-sleeved shirt. The school-sponsored breakfast programs had no shortage of students sent by their parents to have a free meal before the start of the school day. The community's economic realities left very few options for those struggling to make ends meet.

As the saying goes, "desperate times call for desperate measures." At a young age, many made the decision to improve their circumstances by securing an education, while others attempted to escape the perception of their doomed fate by getting involved in petty theft and other crimes to achieve their desired lifestyle. It was difficult to see people in the surrounding affluent communities enjoying the finer things of life and not want them for yourself. The temptation to make the wrong decision was something we all faced. A poor choice usually led to an arrest, a criminal record, and a foregoing of future career opportunities. For one to truly understand the issues, it is important to have a historical perspective of the area. Growing up in Jane and Finch, I can only account for what I personally witnessed as a child. Years later as an adult, I would come to learn and understand the root of the problems that continue to plague the community today.

Anastasiya Romanska, in her article entitled "The History of the Jane and Finch Neighbourhood in Toronto," highlighted that in the 1960s, the original intention of the Ontario Housing Corporation (OHC), along with the North York Planning Department, was to develop a new "instant community" as a model suburb and solution to Toronto's rapid growth. However, experts suggest that OHC did not properly consider the social infrastructure that would be needed to sustain such a community. In the years to follow, a row of high-rise apartments was built along Jane Street, which would become known as the "Jane and Finch corridor." With most of its steadily growing population in low-income and public housing, the community became known for its high levels of poverty.

According to Inner City Outreach, one of the neighbourhood's not-for-profit organizations, "By the mid-1970's, several social issues surfaced from the rapid growth of the community and large concentrations of low-income households. The area soon became notorious for its prevalence of gangs, drugs, and criminal activity." My objective is not to get into an academic debate about these findings but to simply provide some context for those unaware of the area and shed light on some of the external challenges I was facing as a youth.

I remember being genuinely excited when my parents first proposed moving to the Jane and Finch community. Leaving downtown Toronto presented an opportunity to explore a new part of the city and make new friends. This was a moment in my life that I was ready to seize. I was eagerly searching to find myself and feel connected to something that felt familiar. However, my idyllic vision of living out childhood bliss would be rudely interrupted by systemic barriers, setbacks, and emotional pain that made my experience less than ideal.

At the beginning, our new community was everything I had hoped for. As proud new homeowners, we opened the front door at 156 Eddystone Avenue. Immediately, I noticed that our three-story condominium unit was much larger than our previous rented apartment. With four bedrooms and two bathrooms, we had more space to navigate without constantly bumping into each other.

Eager to learn more about the building, I took every elevator and every staircase, curious to see where they would lead. What I found was paradise. There was a party room, weight room, and a sauna in the basement. I later discovered a large swimming pool at the back of the building. For a while, it felt like my family had won the lottery. For the first few months, there was no reason to leave the building. I had all the amenities I needed. My only wish was to enjoy what I had found with some new friends.

In my search for companions, it turned out I did not have to look far. My Jamaican family's unit was sandwiched between a Vietnamese couple on the left and a Serbian family on the right. After getting to know the parents and their respective sons, Tien and Sergan, the boys immediately became my best friends. We would frequently rotate between each other's homes, watching movies and trading hockey cards. Dinners during the week ranged from tasty cuisines from Southeast Asia to dishes from Europe and, of course, Jamaica. The variations in our upbringing, race, and religion did not prevent us and our families from bonding. Our differences and similarities enriched our friendship. Without travelling the world, I was learning more about places I had never been, just through my daily interactions with them.

Unbeknownst to me at the time, I was learning key lessons on how families, friendships, and communities can be forged when we decide to set aside the artificial barriers amongst us. I would later meet a group of friends in the building, spanning from across the globe. There was Sanjay from India, Ricardo from Trinidad, and Larry from Italy, affectionately known as "Big Dog" for his booming voice. We were playfully known as the United Nations gang. In some ways, we had the characteristics of a gang. We spent a lot of time together, and there was nothing I would not do to help a member of the group in need. It was more than friendship; they were family. At that point in my life, my friendships were a welcomed distraction from the personal struggles I was having with my own family. Unfortunately, life as I knew it was going to change drastically.

Over the next few months, I noticed that our perfect building was changing rapidly. It first started with the closure of the party room. Within weeks, the weight room and sauna were permanently closed. I began hearing whispers that illicit behaviour was the main reason for the closures. The final kick in the gut was the closure of the swimming pool. With the building amenities gone, I was forced to consider other options to occupy my time.

Young and curious, it was time to venture outside my comfort zone and see what else the community had to offer. I was startled to learn what was lurking just yards away from my safe confines. In broad daylight, I witnessed things that no young child should have to encounter. There was drug dependency, gang violence, and a noticeable police presence. Any movement outside of my home had to be planned and calculated. I was forced to navigate my community with surgical precision to avoid ending up in spaces and circumstances that could get me into trouble. Only months away from my eleventh birthday and I was already developing "street smarts." I quickly learned the skill of minding my own business. I dared not to question or report the illegal activities that I saw. By this time, I was already hearing stories of what happened to those who were labelled as "neighbourhood snitches."

With each passing day, it became clear that the illegal activities I had seen had entered my building. It was the reason for the closures of the amenities that I, and other families, had once enjoyed. In my former community, I was never exposed to the frightening elements I was now encountering. The rough edges of Jane and Finch arrested my attention, along with those living outside the community. It was here that I first learned how socioeconomic disparities, a lack of resources, and a negative community reputation could impact your daily experiences and future opportunities.

Sports became the easiest way for me to connect with the wider community. It was also a way to stay out of trouble. I never told my parents or my siblings what I had observed in the neighbourhood. My family had moved to the Jane and Finch community to provide us with a better life, and the last thing I wanted to do was cause unnecessary stress.

When I requested to play recreational sports, my parents readily agreed by scraping enough money together for the cost to participate. I enjoyed a cross-section of sports, but my favourite was basketball. As a social child, it did not take me long to bond with my new teammates. In time, I discovered that many of them were also witnessing the darker elements of our community.

For most of us, it was obvious that sports had become a temporary escape from our surroundings. As time went on, we learned that the everyday challenges in the community were much bigger than ever imagined. To our surprise, the sport that provided us with a sacred refuge would now be impacted by the stereotypical views held by those outside of our community. When teams from surrounding neighbour-hoods were scheduled to play at our local gyms, it was not uncommon to hear opposing coaches sending notices of regret, citing safety con-cerns. In other words, they were worried about being attacked, robbed, or something worse. We were far from criminals or gang bangers. We were all innocent kids who simply loved the game of basketball and the spirit of competition. It was heartbreaking and very difficult not to take it personally.

Suddenly, the innocence of playing a sport we all enjoyed was gone, and we were now fighting to establish our reputation and value, both on and off the court. So when teams were willing to play us, we went out of our way to prove that we were normal kids just like any other. No trouble, no yelling at the referees, and always displaying professional sportsmanship. Any slip up would immediately justify the stereotypes that had been cast on us. At times, it honestly felt as though we were doing auditions every time we stepped on the court. Instead of playing for the love of the game, I was becoming resentful of the way we were being perceived and the fact that it was left to us to prove people wrong. Unfortunately, I soon learned that the negative perception of our community had spread far beyond sports. It had also entered our schools. As a student, I would hear teachers complain about the lack of resources, crime, and their bitterness about being sent to our community as a form of punishment. A transfer to a school in

Jane and Finch was seen as detrimental to one's career. While many students were up late studying for exams, it appeared that some teachers were also up devising plans to leave the community at the first available opportunity. With the revolving door of teachers, the right to receive quality education was in jeopardy. While I acknowledge that there were teachers who were committed to the students and the community, as a youth, it was difficult to ignore the negative comments and the impact they had on many of us.

Despite the everyday struggles and challenges growing up in Jane and Finch, I strongly resisted the fearmongering and the belief that our community possessed no value. I was disappointed to see the willingness of many to turn a blind eye to the positive aspects of the community. Unlike some of Toronto's more celebrated communities, which highlighted wealth and prestige, the Jane and Finch community was unique, in that it was a model of multiculturalism, where many people of various ethnic, racial, religious backgrounds interacted, played, and worked with each other. Even with the positive features of the community on full display, the message was clear: A predominantly racialized community doing good things was not worthy of favourable news coverage.

Although the negative labelling had its impact on how many of us were perceived, it did not overshadow the formation of early friendships and experiences that played a significant role in my character development. I saw the value of sharing my lived experiences with those from different backgrounds. I embraced the diversity, unique characteristics, and common belief that we were outsiders from the rest of society. My own experience of feeling disconnected from my family allowed me to easily connect with a group of young men who were also seeking to find their identities and voices in a community struggling for its own acceptance.

The move to Jane and Finch gave me something I had hoped

for—a sense of belonging. It was in this troubled community that I first developed a clear picture of my worth and conviction, refusing to be defined by the standards and expectations of others. I finally took pride in cultivating my own experiences and stories rather than attempting to walk in someone else's shoes. Instead of running away from my insecurities, I developed the courage to address them head-on. Through self-evaluation and reflection, I could smile back at what I saw in the mirror.

It took time and an unexpected change in circumstances to arrive at a place of self-acceptance. My family and friends accepted me with no strings attached. Despite what was happening around me, I was finally getting my footing and a measure of confidence. Unfortunately, a sudden departure in my family would have me searching to find myself yet again.

Chapter 2

Setbacks Are Not an Excuse for Failure

"There are only two options: make progress or make excuses."

– Steve D. Anderson

A LONG LIFE'S JOURNEY, it is inevitable that we will experience setbacks and disappointments. It is how we respond to these experiences that shapes our character and trajectory in life. I was just getting comfortable with myself and my new community when I was forced to deal with a blow that threatened to erase all the progress I had made.

The incident I am referring to is my parents divorce. It is generally understood that the impact of divorce between a couple can reverberate for generations. While it is true that divorce is traumatizing for the separating parties, I believe children are often impacted the hardest, having yet to develop the emotional maturity or capacity to cope. It is not uncommon for children to question whether they had something to do with the separation. Some will become withdrawn from their social network of friends and activities, as they struggle to control their feelings. There are moments of shame, especially when children are asked about their parents', or when they overhear others happily discussing their own. Avoidance of these situations certainly prevents an exacerbation of the pain.

The inability to handle the stress of an uprooted home environment can lead to unintended consequences. Not getting the professional assistance I needed to help cope with my emotions, directly contributed to poor decisions in key moments of my life.

The Blind Side

Decades have passed since the divorce of my parents, but I still vividly recall the feeling of shock that ran through my body the moment I found out. I was in Grade 7 and the ripe age of twelve, when my life took a dark turn. The day was like any other, and I was eager to come home from school to watch some of my favourite cartoons. My routine was simple: get home, kick off my shoes, and grab the TV remote. I would first watch an episode of *G.I. Joe*, then *Transformers*, before grabbing something to eat and eventually doing my homework.

As I opened the front door, I sensed something was different. I was surprised to see my mom sitting on the couch. She was usually at work and would often work a few hours of overtime to help make ends meet. Therefore, seeing her home at this time raised alarm bells, and I immediately suspected something was wrong. Before I could muster another thought, I glanced at her face only to see a stream of tears. My mind immediately jumped to a thousand scenarios of what could be the cause of her sadness. I attempted to ask one of the million questions running through my mind, but I could not get out a word.

A voice in my head told me to head upstairs and enter her bedroom. As I approached the front doors of the bedroom, I immediately noticed the closet door was open and empty of all my father's belongings. Not a single item was left behind. He was careful not to leave a trace of his existence in our home.

Shell shocked by what I had discovered, my mind could not think rationally. Despite what my eyes had seen, I refused to accept the outcome. Instead, I pursued other plausible reasons for the empty closet. Perhaps something happened to him. Maybe he was taken to the hospital and took his clothes with him. It was wishful thinking, but it was easier to accept. For what felt like hours, I scanned the entire room, thinking this was all a bad dream. Thoughts continued to swirl in my head as to what could have happened. Finding no sensible answers to my questions, I was forced to settle on the reality that my father had packed up and left our home for good. Only a short time ago, we had left our tiny apartment in Toronto and moved to Jane and Finch for a better life, and now that was destroyed.

I was completely blindsided by what I had discovered, and by the look on my mother's face, it was clear that she was, too. From my perspective, our family was like any other. There were the occasional disagreements and spirited discussions, but nothing that would have led to this sudden conclusion. My parents had gone through a lot and sacrificed so much to provide us with the opportunities they never had. It was a struggle, but our family always found a way to get through the difficult times together. The reality that an important member of the household was now gone was hard to fathom. How were we going to manage? For the first time in my life, I felt our big, proud, loving, and stable Jamaican family had been shattered.

At only twelve years old, I was left to ponder many questions. How would I explain this to my friends? How would I be viewed? How would the rest of my family react? What did this mean for our family? As much as I wanted to know right away, I knew my questions would be eventually answered in time. I dreaded the unknown.

Recognizing that my mother needed my attention, I slowly came downstairs, hoping to never reach the bottom. In the living room, I sat with her in complete silence. Although I wanted to be a source of support, I did not have the words to comfort or reassure her in that moment. I lapsed back into my own thoughts, trying to find a way to deal with what I was feeling.

Slowly, the rest of my family came home to learn the devastating news. There was no formal family discussion. Understandably, there was not much to say, and I did not feel like talking. Without having any say in our father's decision, our lives were suddenly turned upside down, affecting us all in different ways. From that day on, we collectively avoided discussing the topic, a decision I believe deprived us of the healing we needed.

My father's decision to leave our family was extremely difficult, but to add insult to injury, he did so without the courtesy of leaving a note. I believe that if he had sat down with our family, reasoned with us, provided his explanation for leaving, we could have come to terms with and, perhaps, even accepted his decision. My mother's tears and our inability to change his decision was unforgivable. The first few weeks after his departure were particularly difficult because of the looming uncertainty in all our lives. Prior to the separation, I was usually joyful, hopeful, and optimistic for the future. It did not take long for a darker side to emerge. I became easily agitated and found myself getting upset over the most trivial things. I was not myself, but I did not care. This was my way of dealing with the separation.

Shockingly, three months later, before the dust of his departure could clear, my dad reached out to my older brother Chester and me, wanting to connect. Why us? Why not the rest of my siblings? I can only imagine that he chose the both of us because we were the youngest in the family, only two years apart in age. After several calls back and forth, my mother reluctantly agreed that we could pay him a visit. I believe that she, along with my brother and I, had a glimmer of hope that things could be restored.

Figure 2.1: My brother Chester and I standing at High Park

My dad picked us up and took us to High Park in Toronto. This was our first time going to High Park, so we got dressed for the occasion. Chester and I were attired in matching yellow jerseys, with the number 10 printed on the front. The entire car ride to the park was awkwardly silent, as my brother and I were still trying to process what was happening. It did not help that our dad had little to say himself.

When we arrived, we walked over to a set of picnic benches where he sat us down and attempted to explain his departure and desire to reconnect. He appeared convincing about wanting to be present in our lives, again. We listened attentively, and my hardened heart began to slightly soften with each promising word he spoke. We had a good day, as my dad indulged us with food and plenty of assurances that things would get better. We both arrived home cautiously optimistic about the future with our dad. With confidence, he declared he would call again shortly, and we could look forward to another great outing.

Unfortunately, it did not take long before it all came crashing down, again. The follow-up phone call never came, and it was clear that the interest from my dad had been short-lived. Once again, we were left without any explanation. It was more painful than the initial departure, because I had allowed myself to be vulnerable, to let my dad back into my life, and to think of what was possible.

For a long time, it was a bitter pill to swallow, as I had looked up to my dad as a source of strength. He had always commanded respect from our family and his peers. I hoped to one day stand in his shoes, garnering the same level of respect. My father was a hard-working, blue-collar worker who drove a truck for a living. I vividly recall him driving his yellow company truck home and parking it in front of our building. It was a source of pride to tell my friends that the truck they saw outside belonged to my dad. For a period, I, too, wanted to drive a truck just to be like him.

I had fond memories attending my dad's work Christmas parties with my brother Chester, where we would sit at his table, waiting for the arrival of the toys and other items to our liking. My father was generous, charismatic, and funny, all attributes I desired. Unfortunately, his influence would be severed by his abrupt departure from our household. I promised never to open that door again, to avoid further pain.

As time passed, I felt the need to step up and help around the house. I began looking for work to help offload the burden suddenly placed on my mother. She never once asked for help, and if I told her about my intentions, I knew she would have flatly refused. It was best that I kept my job search a secret.

Although very young, I was tall for my age and, therefore, looked older in the eyes of those who did not know me. I prayed earnestly that someone would see my desire to work and extend me an opportunity. The answer to my prayers came a few weeks later in the form of a paper route. I was over the moon and excited to tell my family that I was now gainfully employed. I took pride in knowing that, in some small way, I could help fill the gap my father had left behind.

Every weekend, I delivered the newspaper to two nearby buildings after completing my own. I would earn barely over one hundred dollars every two weeks, but I was sure to give my mother at least fifty dollars. Each time, my mother took the money with a smile, followed by a kiss on the cheek. I was doing my part, and I was happy for it. A few years later, I learned that my mother had taken every dollar and opened a savings account. It was not much, but it was money I could access in the future when I needed it.

Work was a welcomed distraction from the pain of my own emotions. The distraction did not last very long, as I was in store for some more devastating news. While I enjoyed delivering the newspaper, it was often difficult to get people to pay for what they owed. I tried my hardest to collect what was outstanding, but because of my age, I was not taken seriously.

One Sunday morning, I was preparing the papers for delivery when I heard an unexpected knock on my front door. When I opened it, I was surprised to see the District Manager who had hired me. I immediately recognized him. He was very tall with long, sandy blonde hair that he always wore in a ponytail. Before I could invite him in, he confidently entered, and we both headed for the living room. We were seated for only for a minute before he started to explain that I had not collected enough money over the past several weeks. I tried to articulate the best I could the difficulties I was encountering, when he interrupted me and said, "Steve, do you know what this means?" Fearful to respond, I said nothing. He went on to say, "You are fired."

What? Fired? I was trembling and could not come up with a word in response. Just like that, my boss-no-more collected my papers and my receipt book and left the house as quickly as he had entered. I sat motionless in the living room, not knowing what to say or think. I had just gotten fired in my own home. I was certain that I was the only kid that that had ever happened to in the whole world. I was embarrassed to tell my family of my fate. I eventually told them days later that I had quit because I needed more time to focus on school. I knew it was a lie and the wrong thing to do, but I could not stomach being the butt of inevitable jokes. With my confidence shaken, I did not look for work again until years later.

I was starting to crumble, believing that life as I once knew it would never be the same, again. There was no rainbow around the corner. Life showed me no mercy, as my world was about to be rocked, again.

Finding Comfort in the Wrong Places

In my household, I often heard my mother say, "When it rains, it pours." As a child, I never fully understood the meaning of this statement, but now it made all the sense in the world. Major disappointments in my life were happening in rapid succession. My parents had separated, the attempt by my father to establish a relationship with my brother and me post-separation had failed miserably, and I had been fired from my first job.

My sense of value hit rock bottom, and I was embarrassed to face my family and friends. They were always supportive when I needed them the most, but I was convinced that I no longer deserved to be in their company. I veered away from my core group of friends and found company with another group headed in the wrong direction. Instead of ambitious, positive, and forward-thinking individuals, I was now surrounded by school dropouts, thriving off the gains of street life.

My new friends were very eager to exploit my pain, anger, and frustration. It did not take long before the grooming process began. Each day after school, I was routinely pressured to carry out activities to demonstrate my loyalty to the group. Mad at the world, I consented without considering the potential consequences. It was now official. I had become the person I was desperately trying not to be. When my family moved to the Jane and Finch community, I did my best to avoid associating with people on the wrong side of the tracks, and here I was now, an inducted member. It was a painful reminder of how life can change in an instant, despite your best intentions.

I was often nervous and uneasy about what I had witnessed in the people I had chosen to surround myself with. Drug use, credit card scams, and violence were regular occurrences. Although not directly involved, I was guilty by association. At times, it was hard to believe that this was now part of my life. For many months, I avoided looking into the mirror, knowing it would force me to acknowledge that my behaviour did not represent my true character and how I was raised. My judgment was clouded, but I was determined not to show weakness and vulnerability. The recent experience with my father had taught me how to hide my feelings, fearful that any further expression could lead to more pain. I was changing in plain sight, but my family could not offer much help. They were focused on managing their own emotions following the separation.

Despite the choices I was now making, in my mind I still had things under control. I was not hurting anyone, and I had yet to get into any trouble. My old friends did their best to throw me a lifeline, hoping to steer me back to my previous lifestyle. At the time, I was not ready to be rescued. It would take a scary event in the mall parking lot to give me a glimpse of how far I had departed from the life I once enjoyed.

One day after school, I stuck around to play basketball in the gym with some of my classmates. After finishing, I walked a short distance to the Jane and Finch Mall to meet up with some of my new neighbourhood friends. We spent the rest of the afternoon, well into the evening, walking and chatting with people we knew and recognized in the mall. Oblivious to the time, we were all surprised to hear the announcement over the P.A. system that the mall would be closing in ten minutes. We proceeded to the exit and opened the doors to see that the sun had been replaced by the night sky.

Before the doors could close behind us, flashing blue and red lights illuminated our faces.

Before I could figure out the source of the lights, I witnessed two members of our group being surrounded and violently taken to the ground by two large men wearing police uniforms. It all happened in a matter of seconds. I was close to being arrested, and it rattled me. I stood silent and frozen on the spot, as I saw my friends placed in the back of the cruiser and whisked out of sight. Those of us who remained quickly dispersed without saying a word, not knowing if the police would come back to get us.

I went home and straight to my room to avoid contact with my family. I could never bring myself to share what had just happened. The next day, I learned that a store clerk at the mall had recognized two of the guys I was with and had tipped off the police regarding their alleged involvement in a massive credit card scam. It dawned on me that I had narrowly escaped the long arm of the law that devoured so many Black youths in the Jane and Finch community.

I admit that in my short time with my new group, the temptation to participate in similar and other lucrative activities was real, but something always kept me from crossing the line. Upon reflection, I am confident that the prayers of my mother had kept me safe and out of serious trouble.

For many nights, I tossed and turned, unable to sleep as I relived the close encounter at the mall that almost changed my life forever. In moments of clarity, I was deeply ashamed of myself and fearful of the disappointment I would cause my family if I got arrested. I was a good child from a good family. My mother was an excellent role model. I had wonderful siblings. How could I become a near criminal despite what I had? Day to day, I was dangerously close to falling into the stereotypical narrative of growing up in a rough neighbourhood and inevitably devoting myself to a life of crime. I had taken several steps back from the person I was shaping up to be prior to the divorce. Once again, I was falling into the trap of becoming a person I was not meant to be. The arrest of my friends forced me to reflect on the current state of my life and the direction I was headed in. Sadly, I was still hurting, and was not prepared to let go of this new group just yet. But before I could put my near arrest behind me and figure out my next step, I was forced to deal with another major setback.

The Downward Slide Continues. My Experience with ESL

Regardless of what I was going through, I had managed to keep up my studies, with my education being one of the few things that remained unchanged. My grades were always competitive but, admittedly, I struggled with math. The skills I lacked in math, I made up for with my love for reading. With my world crumbling around me, my ability to get immersed in a book brought me comfort. Like sports, reading was a temporary escape from the issues I was facing as a youth. It allowed me to focus on the lives and circumstances of other people rather than my own. The books I read were diverse in subject matter, including famous biographies, ancient history, technology, health, and world wars. My family was amazed by my reading interests and vocabulary at such a young age.

All throughout elementary school, my passion and ability to read beyond my grade level was a point of emphasis by teachers on my report card. After graduating from elementary school at Grade 6, I entered Grade 7 at Oakdale Junior High.

Barely two weeks into school, I was inexplicably placed into ESL for my apparent difficulties with grasping the English language. How could this be? I was born in Canada. I could read, write, and communicate effectively. At this point in my life, I had several issues I was struggling with, but expressing myself in a clear and articulate manner was not one of them.

I wondered if the teachers had made a mistake. Perhaps they were referring to another Steve who was new to the country. I could not help but think that I was another victim of the stereotypical views held by educators who had the responsibility to teach and inspire us. I was barely a teenager, and once again I was filled with disappointment and rage that would rival any disgruntled adult.

I had little time to fully understand the reason, as I was hustled off to the new program. Going to a new school and starting Grade 7 was supposed to be a happy time, meeting new people and feeling optimistic about the academic opportunities ahead. Instead, it was mired in shame and embarrassment. Education was the one thing I took pride in, and now that was slipping through my fingers. I was drowning in fear and disappointment, but I decided to deal with this issue alone. After all, my mother and siblings already had a lot on their plate following the divorce. I could not bear to burden them with anything more.

Each morning in homeroom, all my classmates gathered to hear the morning announcements and instructions from the teacher before heading out to our respective classes. It was always lively, as we would trade stories and share our plans for the day. Then, like a scene in a horror movie, there was a loud knock on the door and sudden silence, as everyone turned around to see who was there. I lost all the colour in my face when I saw that it was my ESL teacher. I had not told any of my classmates about this embarrassing setback. It was my full intention to keep this highly sensitive matter a secret. I had assumed that after homeroom, I could disappear into that class without being noticed. The proverbial cat was now out of the bag, and I was not ready for the moment.

My teacher entered the room with intrigue and suspense following his every movement. It was my worst nightmare. He walked towards me, stopping several steps short before calling out my name. For the first time in my life, I wished that I were invisible.

He then proceeded to escort me out of the classroom. The walk of shame was unbearable as I could hear the laughter and whispers of my fellow students, with some going as far as to ask where I was going. Before I could fully exit the room, I heard the teacher say, "Steve is on his way to the ESL program, and he will join all of you later."

My mood immediately turned sour, because I was made to feel different from everyone else. I felt like a defected toy that was not good enough to join the new products on the display shelf. Fitting in and finding a sense of belonging was something I had struggled with growing up. Here I was again, fighting to not feel different. This became the routine every morning, and the sting of each occasion was as potent as the first.

I could not believe how dramatically my life had turned around in just a year. The temptation to give up was a recurring voice in my head that refused to go away. Never known to be a quitter, I hung in there, searching and praying for a glimmer of hope. I was desperate for a change in my circumstances. Little did I know that unexpected help, from a person I never wanted to see, was on the way.

The daily trek to the ESL room was a painful reminder of my downward trajectory. I can still visualize the often cold and dimly lit room. What was supposed to be a classroom felt more like an interrogation room. I thought I would be joined by other students, but none ever came.

Without the distraction from other students, I had a lot of time to engage in my own thoughts. I kept telling myself that I was born in Canada to English-speaking parents. I was a good student. I was well-spoken, fluent in English, and could read with a high level of comprehension. Why was I here? Had the educational system capped my potential before giving me the opportunity to see how high I could reach? The frustration, anger, and self-pity I felt for being placed in ESL surprisingly began to ease when I got to know my ESL teacher, Mr. Lynn.

Mr. Lynn was Caucasian with piercing blue eyes. He was a short man, standing barely five feet tall. What he lacked in height, he made up with his confidence and positive attitude. From the start, Mr. Lynn saw my ability and who I could become. He never considered my race, ethnicity, or background as the reason for being placed in ESL. Instead, his main goal was to empower anyone he worked with to become a better student and eventually transition from ESL. He had no patience for self-loathing, excuses, or failure without effort. On the way to his classroom every morning, he would say, "It's time to work." He constantly repeated the phrase, "Never be limited and confined by your current circumstances. If you want to change it, you must work hard to do just that."

From the moment I was assigned to him, I could feel my confidence slowly starting to return. He pushed me with such conviction within the one-hour period that my confidence was eventually restored. I was determined to work my way out of ESL at the same speed at which I had entered. Initially, it was assumed that I would be in Mr. Lynn's class for the rest of the year to work out my alleged deficiencies. However, in short order, it became crystal clear to Mr. Lynn and me that I did not belong in ESL. I was there for barely a month when I heard the words that I would never forget, "Steve, you don't belong in ESL, and I am recommending you be placed in Advanced English."

You said what?

I looked over my shoulder to make sure he was not talking to someone else who had entered the room. "Say that again," I said, softly, wanting to make sure that my ears were not deceiving me.

With a louder voice, Mr. Lynn repeated, "You don't belong in ESL, and I am recommending you enter advanced English."

You can only imagine how I felt. Just like that, I was leaving the ESL program and heading directly to advanced English. My teacher's words validated how I had felt about myself academically for quite some time.

Before I could descend from my emotional high, Mr. Lynn began writing his letter of recommendation and directed me to the school's main office. It honestly felt as if I had been given the keys to get out of jail. I do not recall whom I ran over or elbowed on my way out of the classroom, but I likely set a Canadian sprinting record in my dash to the office. Upon arrival, I opened the front doors and proceeded to the front desk with all the confidence in the world. I was certain that I would be sitting in an advanced English classroom that afternoon. Unfortunately, that belief would be derailed, albeit temporarily.

I happened to see the guidance counsellor walking to her desk. With all the strength and confidence in my voice, I said, "Excuse me, my name is Steve, and I am here from Mr. Lynn's classroom." She immediately turned around and stared directly at me, apparently aggravated that I had disturbed her. Undeterred by her unwelcoming presence, I blurted out, "Mr. Lynn said I shouldn't be in ESL and recommended my transfer to Advanced English at the next available opportunity."

With a firm voice, she proceeded to ask for my student number and headed towards the filing cabinet to retrieve my school records. I remember her rifling through my file, turning each page with the lick of her finger. After what felt like an eternity, she turned and said, "Steve, I have reviewed your file, and despite what Mr. Lynn has said, I believe you're a C student at best." This blow was followed with, "If you want to formally have your status changed, you must have a parent come in and sign off on this."

I left the office stunned, hurt, and in disbelief. However, I was not going to let this encounter shake my confidence. I worked hard to get to this point, and there was no turning back.

That evening, I spoke to my mother about the need to have her attend the office to sign some papers. I purposely left out the details of what I had gone through. I knew if she realized the full extent of my experience, she would have come down to school hotter than a Jamaican scotch bonnet pepper. My mother is a petite woman and is normally calm and collected. However, when it came to her children, she could switch on that Caribbean flare in a moment's notice. I had previously witnessed teachers learning the hard way about messing with Caribbean children. For many of our parents, there was no such thing as a quiet, closed-door meeting. The whole school would hear what was going on, even if that conversation originated in the school parking lot.

A part of me wanted to unleash that flare on school officials as a form of revenge, considering what I had been put through. That would have ensured that I would never be placed in ESL again. However, it was not time for revenge; it was time to move forward.

The next morning, my mother made the necessary arrangements at work, and we walked together to school. Along the way, I was praying that my fortune had not changed from the day before. I began to worry. Had Mr. Lynn changed his mind? Would the principal override Mr. Lynn's recommendation? Would they require more information from my mother and me? Considering how quickly my life had changed after moving to Jane and Finch, it was feasible that it could happen again.

Thankfully, as we entered the main office, my mother was presented with the papers, which we both signed. With the scribble of a pen, I was placed in Advanced English. I went on to complete Advanced English and, subsequently, graduated from Oakdale Junior High in the academic stream geared toward university studies. This experience taught me at an early age that life's obstacles only remain if you allow them. If you are determined and hardworking, anything is possible.

Does that mean that a strong work ethic will allow certain individuals to overcome the trappings of prejudice and systemic barriers? No. Will some people try to hold you back from reaching your full potential? Yes. However, we all have choices in life, and at the time, I chose to fight for my academic future rather than accept the limitations imposed on me.

Despite bouncing back from my experience in ESL, I was still hanging with the wrong company after school. That poor decision threatened to erase the academic gains and future opportunities I was fighting so hard for.

Chapter 3

Show Me Your Company and I Will Tell You Who You Are

*"The better you are at surrounding yourself with people of high
potential, the greater your chance of success."*
– John C Maxwell

IN OUR EARLY years, some of our most significant decisions in life
are influenced by our social network of friends. We are often told
about the importance of finding the right job, spouse, and place to live.
Although these points of emphasis are sound thinking, we seldom give
as much attention to the importance of young people choosing the right
friends or acknowledging the major implications such decisions can have.

In some instances, our friends are closer to us than our family members. We spend the most time with them and often feel comfortable
revealing our true, authentic selves. Significant power and influence are
wielded in these relationships. Therefore, if made correctly, the decision can elevate your life beyond what you can imagine. On the other
hand, if made incorrectly, your choice can lead to failed expectations
and a life of misery.

Whether we like it or not, we cannot ignore the truth that we are defined, judged, and labelled by the company we maintain. On occasion, I would hear my mother say, "Show me your friends and I will tell you who you are." She was right. For periods of time in my youth, my selection of friends was like a mirror revealing exactly who I was at the time. Looking back, I can see that many of my decisions in key phases of my life were based on my network of friends.

Continuing with the Wrong Crowd

Following the separation of my parents, I hitched my wagon to a new set of friends who were far from positive role models. Many wore their numerous run-ins with the law as badges of honour to be celebrated. Despite witnessing some of my friends arrested at the Jane and Finch Mall, I was still hurting and unwilling to walk away from these negative influences. I had become submerged within the group, with a semblance of the old Steve barely hanging on to a life raft.

I was now fifteen years old, and I was already experiencing something akin to a mid-life crisis. I spent many evenings with my gang of friends, walking aimlessly through the neighbourhood, never finding what we all really needed—help. We all had our own grievances towards family, educators, the police, and anyone else who, we felt, had done us wrong. We were young, angry, and misguided, and trouble never seemed too far away. Unfortunately for us, the police also spent many nights patrolling the same streets and did not hesitate to let us know they were monitoring our presence. Marked and unmarked cruisers would follow and track our every movement. It was not unusual to be stopped and questioned about our motives for being out late. It is possible they were just doing their job, but I felt harassed, and my resentment towards them grew with each encounter.

In many respects, I had become the real-life embodiment of Dr. Jekyll and Mr. Hyde. This expression refers to persons with an unpredictably dual nature: outwardly good, but sometimes shockingly bad. I worked hard in school and took pride in my academic abilities and pursuits, but as soon as school was over, I was steadily walking the fine line between light and darkness. In the eyes of some in the community, my choice of friends had me destined for one of two paths: early death or jail.

I refused to see what everyone else did. Consequently, my poor selection of friends and related troubles followed me when I graduated from Oakdale Junior High and entered high school at Westview Collegiate.

I was barely into my first semester at my new school when the trouble had already begun. I was making a strong first impression, but not in the way my family had hoped. Once again, I had decided to hitch my wagon to another group of troublemakers, but this time at school. This decision was different, since I was usually good at separating what happened within the school boundaries and my activities on the outside. The lines were now officially blurred.

I was now a magnet for trouble that led to several trips to the principal's office. During my downward descent, there was always a small voice telling me that my actions were wrong, but the urge to lash out was too intoxicating. I was in one fight after another with people my new friends and I did not agree with. Many times, I was simply following the crowd and fighting for no logical reason of my own. However, at that point in my life, no reason was required.

One day during lunch, I decided to follow some of my school friends who'd decided to use force to resolve a disagreement with another group of boys on school property. Although not directly involved in the physical altercation, I was pointed out by by-standers as being part of the group. Following an investigation by school officials, I was subsequently suspended for three days. I was guilty by association. I had officially hit rock bottom.

Prior to my suspension, I had been good at avoiding the consequences of my actions. In some ways, I felt empowered by this invincibility. Truthfully, it was only a matter of time before I had to face the weight of my actions, and that time had come. My downward slide was now complete.

Oddly, in my defiance stage, I was more concerned about the punishment at home than I was about the actual suspension. In most Caribbean households, it was not uncommon to hear your parents say, "If you bring the police or trouble to my door, watch what I am going to do to you." When translated, this meant a thick black belt and a loss of skin on some part of your body. The punishment was rarely carried out, as the warning was enough to deter the potential of bad behaviour. However, things were different. I was different. I knew the school had called my mother at work and told her about my suspension. Before she got home, I hid in the closet, hoping to diffuse her anticipated anger. I went from a hardened young man walking the streets late at night to a boy now cowering in the closet. Believe me when I say that the fear of a Caribbean parent can make you do that.

To my surprise, my decision to stay out of my mom's way worked. I did not receive the punishment I had expected. I was fortunate to avoid a spanking but could not escape the lecture of throwing my life away due to poor choices. My mom's eyes, and her speech, made it clear that I had disappointed her, and that was more painful than any spanking I could have received and deserved.

I spent the second and third day of my suspension reflecting, concluding that a change had to occur for the better. I was determined not to become another poor Black statistic in the Jane and Finch community. My mother always told me that I was special, that I would make a difference in this world. I wanted that for myself, but I needed additional guidance. Like in previous times of despair, help was on its way, again.

Shortly after I returned from my suspension, I met Ian Daley, Andrew Guy, Jeff Lindo, Josiah I, and Maurice Innis. This set of friends helped to change the direction of my life.

Ian, who would become my best friend, also attended Westview, and we met in my second semester gym class. Jeff, Andrew, and Josiah had all recently moved into my building on Eddystone Avenue. I was first introduced to them by a friend who thought we would hit it off, considering we had similar qualities. From that moment, we became inseparable. Having not seen them before my suspension, it appeared that God had revealed them to me at a time I needed a fresh start. I would later meet Maurice at a church I began attending closer to home.

It did not take long for me to see that these guys were different from my troubled friends, many of whom were always talking about the next big scheme and how to get quick cash. Their impact was immediate. It was refreshing to engage in enlightening conversations for a change. Like most teenagers, they liked to have a good time, but they had a limit, often demonstrating a maturity of much older adults. They spoke openly about the struggles of living in the Jane and Finch community and the discipline required to be successful.

I admired the positivity of this ambitious group. They were de-termined not to allow the challenges and barriers prevalent in the community to be an excuse not to succeed. It was common to hear talk about becoming a doctor, lawyer, or owning a business empire. There were no run-ins with the law, criminal records, or school suspensions. My friends were articulate and driven.

When my old street friends began to see my transformation, I was often mocked for the way I now spoke around them, and jeered for thinking about success outside of our community. For them, I was trying too hard to be like the "white man." On several occasions, I was accused of being a "sell out" for not maintaining the code of the streets. These people had spent significant time cultivating me, and now they were starting to feel that I was a wasted investment. I quickly learned to keep my thoughts to myself, in fear of further ridicule.

Escaping their clutches would not be easy; it would take time to completely step away from their influence. I was grateful that my current selection of friends made me feel comfortable being myself. With each passing day, I was being elevated by those who were like-minded. At a very young age, I was determined to succeed, but I was getting in my own way with poor decision-making. I was now surrounded by young men accustomed to making all the right moves, and I was determined to do the same.

My time at Westview Collegiate was short-lived, as my mother insisted that I transfer to another school at the end of the school year to avoid getting into further trouble. After researching schools in the area, I settled on the decision to attend C.W. Jefferys. By all accounts, the school had a solid reputation for preparing students for university. I was excited but nervous about another fresh start.

However, my move to a new school would not be as difficult as I thought, since my best friend, Ian, decided to transfer with me. In my heart, I was confident that Ian's decision, in large part, was based on his desire not to see me reverse the gains I had accomplished in just a few months. I was starting to turn my life around, but it was still early in the transition. Ian had the unique ability to sense when someone needed help and was always there to deliver. I had never met such a willing and patient listener. He truly wanted the best for people, and that included me.

I regularly kept in touch with the other guys, not wanting to lose the connections made. Our friendships lasted and thrived because we were committed to developing one another. Choosing to be aligned and empowered by this core group was one of the best choices I had made in quite some time.

As youths growing up in the Jane and Finch community, we had dreams that many would have said were unrealistic and farfetched, considering the reputation of the area. Fortunately, when you have friends who are supportive and bring out the best version of you, anything is achievable. Presently, Ian Daley is a Senior Prosecuting Lawyer with the Real Estate Commission of Ontario. Andrew Guy is a successful motivational speaker, author, and TEDx speaker. Jeff Lindo is a business owner. And Maurice Innis is a doctor with the Canadian Armed forces.

Caroline Picard and Selena Barrientos penned the article, "It's all about finding the Yin to your Yang." I find the following quote really captures the essence of the relationship I have with my core friends:

> *"Friendships are born a million different ways, and all good friends strive to achieve the same goal to be a source of love and support. Finding a true friend feels like a gift that keeps on giving, even when they are a thousand miles away. Through stressful classes, figuring out a career, and inevitable breakups, our best friends have been there. Whether you are celebrating life or happen to experience an unexpected bump, you can always rely on your friends to be there for you. A listening ear, a shoulder to cry on, or finding the silver lining in a less than ideal situation, all of it means the world to you simply knowing you have your friends supporting you every step of the way."*

Your choice of friends is one of the most important decisions in your life. Great friends are those who motivate you, hold you accountable, support you, and, most importantly, allow you to be yourself. Choose wisely and watch your life become elevated to new heights never imagined.

Chapter 4

Learning to be a Leader

"The greatest leader is not necessarily the one who does the greatest things. he or she is the one that gets the people to do the greatest things."
– Ronald Reagan

A T AGE FIFTEEN, I had found great new friends and was slowly putting the rough start I had at Westview Collegiate behind me. A month away from my sixteenth birthday, I experienced another transition starting Grade 11 at my new school, C.W. Jefferys. I was feeling optimistic and ready to explore my new surroundings. I was fortunate to be able to have a fresh start and a renewed sense of confidence. At this point in my life, this step forward was significant, considering I had previously allowed matters out of my control and poor peer associations to cloud my judgment and sense of value. I now had people around me who cared about my personal development. I was routinely told that I was special and possessed leadership qualities. The positive affirmation had me believing that I was a leader in the making.

At the time, I was convinced that leadership was all about achieving personal success. Many youths my age looked to sporting icons such as basketball star Michael Jordan, wanting to resemble that level of achievement. The formula seemed obvious: If I became successful, it would automatically mean that I was a leader destined to be emulated by others. My time at C.W. Jefferys would challenge my narrow perception and teach me a valuable lesson on the many attributes that make a successful leader.

At the beginning of the semester, it was evident that the school was serious about shaping students to become the role models of tomorrow. Messaging throughout the school left little doubt about the importance of clothing and its connection to success. School officials routinely asserted that if you wanted to become a leader, you had to look the part. If you wanted to be taken seriously, your attire was a crucial component. In the beginning, I recall hearing one of my teacher's say, "Whether you like it or not, we are all judged on the way we present ourselves to the world." This stuck with me, because I wanted to be judged based on what I had to offer, not on the negative labelling placed on people in the Jane and Finch community. I was committed to presenting myself to the world as a person of worth. I wanted to be seen as a leader.

Although C.W. Jeffreys stopped short of mandating a uniform dress code, proper clothing was strongly encouraged. This approach was strikingly different from Westview Collegiate, where it was common for me to attend school in oversized sweatshirts, sneakers, and baggy jeans. Admittedly, my clothing was not sophisticated or professional, but I was young and still developing my sense of style. Thinking back, as a young Black boy growing up in Jane and Finch, it was clear that I did not have the freedom to express myself in my choice of clothing without the risk of being labelled as a troublemaker, drug dealer, or gang banger. On any given day, what one wore could have dire consequences, attracting unwanted scrutiny from the police, mall security, and shopkeepers, all of whom had their minds made up about your intentions. Being followed, subjected to intrusive questions and having your bags routinely searched because of the way you looked and dressed was an unfortunate reality for many racialized youths. The perceptions of criminality became a self-fulling prophecy for those who allowed the constant surveillance and labels to shape how they viewed themselves.

Although I am a firm believer in personal responsibility, it is hard to ignore the significant impact of constant negative labelling. Like it or not, the message was clear: If I was going to have any chance of attaining success, I had to first conform to society's version of how a successful leader looked, talked, dressed, and behaved.

At first, it was slightly intimidating to see young men coming to school wearing dress pants, dress shoes, and crisp white shirts and ties. I never dressed up that much even when I attended church with my family. This was new and uncharted territory for me, but I admired the look of confidence in the students who wore these clothes. It was not long before Ian and I ditched the loose-fitting clothes and adopted what was referred to as the "preppy look." As they say, while in Rome, do what the Romans do. Ian and I convinced our mothers that the money for our desired clothing was an investment in our futures. At the time, we were both unemployed, so any attempt at this transition would have failed without family support.

Although my mother was supportive, money was not freely given; it was earned in the Anderson household. It was important that I was taught the value of a dollar from a young age. I performed numerous household tasks and errands to support my chosen lifestyle. It taught me the early lesson not to rely on handouts to obtain the things I wanted in life.

Once Ian and I decided to commit to the new dress code, it was only fitting that we added our own flare to take things up a notch. It was not enough to wear a white dress shirt and tie, we had to accompany our outfits with personalized tie clips and cufflinks. We certainly could not afford the designer clothing often found at the Eaton Centre or

Yorkdale Mall. Instead, Ian and I became skilled negotiators, securing discounts from a little-known Italian clothing store in the Jane and Finch Mall. Looking back, I believe we got favourable deals because the owner was impressed with our commitment to dressing well at such a young age.

Our desire to stand out and get noticed worked. Many took note and began to follow suit. It felt good, for a change, to take the lead on a positive trend. It was less than a year ago that I was trending in the wrong direction, getting suspended from school. This whole experience had a profound impact on my view on clothing and how it presents one to the world. The saying "dress to impress" began to make a lot of sense to me. I was not wealthy by any means, but my new look communicated confidence, intelligence, and a level of importance. The peer feedback Ian and I received on our clothing choices went beyond mere compliments; we were garnering respect, and that was more important. It was an additional boost to our confidence that many of the popular girls were beginning to take notice and whisper our names as we walked by.

The benefits of our new dress code extended beyond the boundaries of school. We also enjoyed the advantages of dressing well when it came to securing employment. If we wanted to maintain our image, we had to find a way to pay for it outside the support of our families. We both began looking for part-time work, casting our nets wide to increase our chances of success. It was Ian who noticed that the United Parcel Service (UPS) located near Jane and Steeles was hiring part-time general labourers to load and unload vehicles. *How hard could it be to lift boxes?* After all, we were young, strong, and energetic, we concluded.

We scraped together enough money and took the bus to attend walk-in interviews that were scheduled throughout the day. We entered the building with our staple look, wearing white dress shirts, ties, cufflinks, dress pants, and our best polished shoes. With every step, we were followed by the curious eyes of employees who assumed we were either management or applying for a management position. We could never have imagined that our choice of clothing would have such an impact outside of the four walls of our school.

Looking back, we were obviously overdressed for the occasion, but we were focused on achieving a singular goal. We both left employed, beating out many other qualified applicants. We would soon exchange our clothes for overalls and work boots, but it did not matter, because we had accomplished our mission. Ian and I were certainly judged on our knowledge during the interview process, but our clothes and how we presented ourselves surely played a significant role in our being hired.

My clothing transformation was not met with approval from all who knew me in the community, as I was once again labelled a "sell out," who was desperate to join the "white establishment." I no longer represented my community's definition of street attire. In some corners, I was now seen as an outsider. At this stage of my life, I was better equipped to handle the criticism, knowing my goal was not, in fact, to represent the "streets." I was more concerned about representing my family and community with honour and integrity in my pursuit for success. I was finally on the right path, so turning back to please others was not an option.

My teachers also saw me differently, but this time, it was with potential and respect. Barely a year earlier, while attending Westview Collegiate, I was viewed by many school officials as a follower and a troublemaker, destined for no good. I could not blame them for having this thought, as I gave them little reason to think otherwise. Could they have been more patient? Maybe. Should they have tried to see what was really going on in my life? Maybe. However, part of growing up is acknowledging your own mistakes.

My new dress code did not elevate me beyond criticism, nor did it shield me entirely from the biases and stereotypes levelled against many Black youths in the Jane and Finch community. However, I saw the early benefits, which resulted in my commitment to stay the course. Being in a new school and recently employed, I was brimming with confidence. I was excited about my future opportunities, but I was still uncertain about the path I would take to achieve my goals. I considered becoming a doctor, a real estate agent, a professional basketball player, an actor, and a TTC bus driver, but it was hard to land on one option.

Growing up in Jane and Finch, I did not see significant attention given to people who left the community and achieved mainstream success. It was not helpful that the media consistently highlighted individuals from the community who were involved in drug and gang activity. Images of Black men from Jane and Finch were relegated to menacing mug shots often displayed on the front page of the Toronto Sun Newspaper for public consumption. Now much older and physically removed from the community, I can see why many did not envision success when thinking about people living in the area. However, at that time, I was determined not to let that perception stop me. I had no choice but to succeed, as the alternative was too painful to accept.

The thought of me driving a transit bus took many of my friends by surprise. It was never a career option discussed amongst us. Quite frankly, I had never heard anyone say they wanted to be a bus driver. My consideration, however, was not by happenstance. My secret infatuation with the TTC began following my parents' move to the Jane and Finch community. Every Saturday morning, my mother would get the entire family ready on time to board the bus. If I had it my way, I would have preferred to sleep in or spend the morning watching cartoons, but that was not meant to be. Honestly, I was a bit resentful at first, considering all my friends would come to school Monday morning talking about the most popular shows. Although I left the house most mornings half-awake, I found pleasure in the one-hour ride to Jane Subway Station. Once on the bus, I would run to the first row of double seats just behind the rear doors. I enjoyed sitting next to the window, watching the cars and people go by. I often attempted to guess the names of each person I saw, while making predictions about where they were going. I was always excited to see what life was like outside of the confines of Jane and Finch. I gave serious thought to one day driving the same TTC 35 Jane Street route and giving passengers the same positive experience I had enjoyed. My fond memories of travelling on the TTC allowed me to keep this employment opportunity as a realistic option.

As I continued my quest towards finding my career choice, one conversation with my Grade 11 law teacher provided the clarity I needed. Law stood out as a subject of intrigue, but I had never fully envisioned myself as a lawyer. Ironically, my older brother Clive was studying to become a lawyer at Osgoode Hall at York University, but that had no real impact on my career choices at the time. At least, so I thought.

My cursory interest in law changed dramatically only a few months into the course. My eagerness and willingness to learn reflected in my grades, as I was consistently scoring near the top of the class. I was a sponge absorbing the legal jargon, theories, and terms found in our readings. Some of my peers were surprised by my early success and the ease with which I grasped the subject. After all, I was Black and over six feet tall. In their eyes, I was destined to play and do well in sports, not academics. No matter how well I dressed to come to class, it could not change how some perceived me.

At times, some of my classmates felt compelled to say, "Steve, you are so tall. You would be an excellent basketball player," or "You probably can run really fast," or "I'm sure with your height you can dunk the basketball." I would always smile, never wanting to show the sting of those comments. It was hard not to notice that those comments were not shared with my fellow Caucasian peers who possessed similar physical traits. Even amongst the marginalized in the Jane and Finch community, there was still a pecking order. I enjoyed the game of basketball, and if I could make a living playing the sport, I would consider myself one of the few privileged ones. However, I refused the labels and the pigeonholing onto an expected path. I would use the remarks as motivation to prove my doubters wrong.

I attended law class every day with an intense focus that usually involved blocking out idle chatter and most of the people around me. To my surprise, I would learn that my teacher was quietly watching my every move. One day after class, I approached my teacher, seeking clarification on a recent assignment. We spoke, and after getting the information I needed, I grabbed my knapsack off my desk and turned to leave the classroom. But the words she uttered stopped me in my tracks and directed my career path from that day forward. She said, "Steve, I have been carefully observing you for the last several months, and my gut tells me you would be a fantastic lawyer, if you continue to stay focused and put in the work necessary." She did not stop there, adding, "The way you speak with confidence, carry yourself, and your commanding presence are all traits of a leader that I see in you."

To say I was shocked would be a gross understatement. With each passing day in the course, I had grown more confident in my abilities, but I never expected such an endorsement. For a moment, I thought I was being pranked, but she spoke with such confidence and conviction that I knew she was serious. Not knowing whether I should smile, laugh, or cry, I stared blankly into her eyes. The moment was very empowering and liberating. Since my arrival in Jane and Finch, I had been fighting to find myself and prove my value. My teacher's comments were proof that I was headed in the right direction. You would have thought this budding lawyer would have supplied a well-crafted response, but I simply said, "Thank you."

I had not received such praise and confidence in my academic abilities in a long time. Just like my ESL teacher, Mr. Lynn, a few years back, my law teacher had communicated a level of confidence that had me walking ten feet tall. It was nice to see my hard work paying off, and that people were starting to take notice. For the remainder of the semester, I continued to put in the work to prove that my teacher's confidence in me was not misplaced. I finished the class knowing exactly what I wanted my future to look like. For the first time, I began to imagine what a career as a lawyer would be. Steve Anderson, Legal Counsel, had a nice ring to it, but I had a long way to go to make that a reality.

Reflecting on the moment, I considered that perhaps I was destined for a career in the legal profession with my older brother Clive, who was already embarking on that path. I also remember my mother's many stories of arriving in Canada alone and petitioning the immigration officials to sponsor my dad and siblings to come from Jamaica. My mother spent a considerable amount of time in the courtroom successfully advocating for the arrival of her family. She proudly recalled her immigration lawyer applauding her preparation and convincing delivery of the evidence during these hearings. It was said that her preparation and credibility played a significant role in my family being reunited in a new country. Her stories made me realize that the seeds of advocacy had already been planted by her heroic actions.

Two lawyers coming from a family in the Jane and Finch community that had been devastated by divorce and financial hardship seemed as real as the tooth fairy. I could only imagine the positive impact on our family and community if my brother and I pulled this off. It would certainly go a long way in challenging the negative perceptions and stereotypes of what is possible for Black youths. Although exciting, I immediately shelved the thought to avoid being distracted from the enormous work ahead.

With the positive affirmations from my friends, and the recent comments from my Grade 11 law teacher, admittedly, my ego began outpacing my humble nature. I was no longer a leader in the making—I was a leader *now*. My confidence had crossed the line into arrogance. I was eager to show that I was a person to be followed now. And my earliest opportunity to demonstrate my leadership abilities was not in the classroom, but on the basketball court. My experience there would end up proving that I still had a lot to learn.

I was almost seventeen years old when I entered Grade 12 at C.W. Jefferys. I spent the first year at my new school working part-time, with the rest of my time focused on my academics. After finishing the year with good grades, I felt comfortable taking on additional responsibilities in the form of basketball. I spent part of the summer playing in tournaments against the best basketball players in the community. The rest of the time, I spent working in a factory with a special someone who was kind enough to get me the job.

My skills were improving with every game played, and people were starting to take notice. When not involved in tournaments, I would spend my Sundays working on my craft, dribbling and shooting on the outdoor basketball courts with my best friend, Ian. He also loved the game, so it was easy to connect on this level. Over the summer, I went through a significant growth spurt, growing from five-feet-eleven to six-feet-three, and my slender frame began to fill out after every workout. My height and build made me suitable for many sports, but my love was basketball. The beginning of the new school year could not come fast enough.

Once the year began, I was still focused on my academics, but I was eager to show off my skills on the court. Finally, the opportunity arrived when the date for basketball tryouts was mentioned during morning announcements. Ian and I met in the cafeteria for lunch that afternoon to discuss trying out for the team. My mind was made up, but I was not sure if he was committed to playing that close to his final year. After a brief discussion and a simple nod of both our heads, the choice was made to take on the challenge together. After two gruelling weeks of outduelling the competition, I was extremely confident that I had made the team, and I did. I was happy to learn that Ian had made the team as well. In our first rounds of practice and exhibition games, I quickly established myself as an offensive powerhouse leading my teammates in scoring.

In my mind, and that of the coaches, I was one of the clear leaders on the team based on my playing abilities. Given that responsibility, many of my teammates looked to me for guidance on the court. I was young, confident, and believed strongly in my leadership abilities. I enjoyed all the recognition and perks that came along with being one of the leaders of the team. For those looking from the outside, I had everything. Although pleased, I was not entirely satisfied. I strongly desired the attention and approval of my older brother Clive who was a legendary basketball player in our community. If there was anyone I wanted to impress, Clive was on the top of my list.

Clive was a standout high school and university basketball player who garnered interest from major basketball programs in Canada and the United States. I admired his ability on and off the court. Not only was he naturally gifted in basketball, but he also displayed the same passion and determination in his academic pursuits.

While studying at Acadia University in Nova Scotia, Clive was presented with the distinguished Student of the Year Award. He was fluent in several languages, easily endearing himself to many around him. He was a leader in the truest sense, with the reputation of making everyone around him better. Chicago Bulls basketball superstar Michael Jordan had a popular Gatorade commercial with the chorus, "Be like Mike. Everyone wants to be like Mike." In our neighbourhood, everyone wanted to be like Clive, and no one wanted to emulate him more than me.

This was my time to prove to Clive that I, too, was a leader. I waited for the biggest game on our schedule against my former school,

Westview Collegiate, to showcase my talents. Clive had never seen me play before, so a lot was riding on my performance. I anticipated a good battle, having played with many of my opponents in summer tournaments. I was excited to rise to the occasion. To the surprise of my friends and teammates, I was not nervous, considering the magnitude of the game. At this early stage of my life, I was used to dealing with high-pressure situations.

As the game approached, I increasingly focused on what I needed to do at the expense of helping my teammates get ready for one of the biggest games of the season. This decision would cost me more than I could have anticipated. The night before the game, I invited Clive to attend, promising him an entertaining match. It was short notice, but he readily agreed. It was indicative of his character. He was well known for showing up for people when needed. If Clive gave you his word, you could count on him to follow through. I went to bed that evening assured that the person I wanted most at the game was going to be there.

The following day, Clive arrived early and sat in the second row of the bleacher seats. He was going to be visible during the entire game, so I was determined to give him a good show. I did, just not the one we both expected. A few minutes before halftime, I was already leading the team in scoring by a landslide, as I had used an array of fast break points, layups, free throws, and three-point shooting to rack up a double-digit scoring total. We were up by twenty points when the coach decided to call a timeout to regroup the team. He feared that we could become complacent with the blowout lead and let our opponents back into the game.

In my mind, the timeout was insignificant in the grand scheme of the game. Little did I know that this minor moment would call into question my notion of leadership. When the timeout whistle blew, rather than joining the team in the huddle, I walked directly to the end of the bench. There I found a spare ball. I picked it up and began to dribble. Instead of paying attention to the coach and encouraging my teammates, I was contemplating how many more points I could get before the end of the game. In my own mind, I did not need to listen to the coach and the other players. After all, I was leading the team in scoring, once again.

My perceived value prevented me from rallying around my teammates. Eventually, we got back onto the floor, finished the second half and eventually our opponent. I finished the game with 34 points, 2 assists, and 6 rebounds. Engulfed in my own accomplishments, I was clueless about the missed opportunity to demonstrate true leadership during the now infamous timeout.

I was proud of my game and assumed that Clive must have been excited to see his little brother rise to the occasion. However, my excitement became confusion when Clive failed to utter a single word the entire car ride home. I recapped the highlights of my performance, hoping it would trigger a response. Not a single word left his mouth. Seriously, not a word! A million thoughts crossed my mind to explain Clive's behaviour, but I could not settle on something that made any logical sense. Disappointed by his muted response, I went straight to my room and remained there for the rest of the day.

The next day, my mother told me that Clive had discussed the game with her. I eagerly yelled, "What did he say?" knowing that he must have told her all about my performance and grand show of leadership. Instead, it was the complete opposite. Rather than heaping praise, he said, "Even though Steve played well, I was embarrassed by his selfishness and disrespect to his coaches and teammates during a timeout. His team won the game, but as one of the leaders on the team, he did nothing to make his teammates better. He seemed determined to impress me rather than putting his teammates in a position to succeed."

He went on to vow that he would never attend another game if I continued with that attitude. I slumped in the living room chair in silence and disbelief as I tried to comprehend what had been said. I could not believe my brother chose to ignore one of my best games of the season and focus on such a trivial matter. Still oblivious to the lesson to be learned, I figured he was mistaken, but it would not take long before I was brought back down to Earth and humbled in one of the biggest moments in my life.

It was only two weeks after hearing Clive's stinging words that our season ended, falling well below expectations. Naturally, I was disappointed, but at the same time I was looking forward to the team's award ceremony. As a consolation, the year would be salvaged with the presentation of the Most Valuable Player award. I was confident that after leading the team in scoring the entire season, the award would certainly be mine. I had already thought about showing off the award to my family and friends, and even decided on a resting place for it in my room. I was most eager to show the award to Clive to prove that his recent assessment of my performance was wrong.

The award assembly was held in our main gymnasium, and it was packed with students across all grades. The players and coaches had already voted on the team awards the day before. I entered the gym and stood near the front. I figured I should sit closer to the stage rather than cut through the crowd to accept my award. That morning, I had re-hearsed the few words I would say after being presented with the award.

Once our head coach had given his speech and overview of the season, it was time to announce the winner. I stood up and began to walk confidently towards the stage, but before I could get there, I heard the name "Freddy Carew." What? I could not believe my ears. I almost fainted.

The moment I realized that the team had declared someone else the MVP, the embarrassment hit. I returned to my seat with my head hung low and in utter disbelief. If there was a big enough hole to crawl into, I would have made a dash for it.

Following the assembly, I went straight to the coach's office to demand an explanation. When I opened the door of his office, his back was turned to me, as he was slowly removing his blazer. Without turning around, he said, "Steve, I know why you are here." It was obvious that he had anticipated my arrival. Eventually, he sat down and proceeded to tell me why Freddy was given the award. He emphasized his leadership qualities on and off the court as justification. The MVP voting was virtually unanimous. Besides me, Ian was the only person on the team that voted for me. Freddy was not the leading scorer on the team; I held that title. My coach acknowledged that scoring was an important consideration but was not everything. Freddy was a fierce competitor, but he also cared deeply about boosting the level of confidence and talent in the people around him. Truthfully, he was also deserving of the award, but at that moment, I found it a difficult pill to swallow. I left the coach's office finally understanding why Clive was disappointed in my lack of leadership on the team.

It was a painful lesson that I sorely needed. If I was going to boldly declare that I was a leader, I needed to act like one. What appeared to be just another basketball timeout turned into a teaching moment that would forever change my outlook. That humbling experience taught me the importance of self-awareness, and how my actions could directly impact others. An effective leader, I learned, is not solely absorbed in his or her own accomplishments but strives to uplift and plant the seeds of leadership in others. Jack Welch, Chairman and CEO of General Electric said it best: "Before you are a leader, success is all about growing yourself; when you become a leader, success is all about growing others." As a person of faith, I am also reminded of the biblical text in Philippians 2:3 which says, "Don't be selfish; don't try to impress others. Be humble, thinking of others as better than yourselves." The whole experience would make me a better person, friend, and leader, with much more to learn.

The irony of this story is that I desperately wanted to be like Clive as a respected leader on the basketball court. While that experience did not turn out the way I had hoped, years later, we would share another platform that would help to transform the image of Jane and Finch for years to come.

Early Reflection

As I consider where I am today, I know that if I could go back in time, I would love to change many things. However, I take comfort that the setbacks made me stronger and wiser, and fuelled my desire to overcome whatever barriers were placed in front of me. Everyone will experience setbacks, but it is important not to dwell on the difficulties. With the right assistance, we can push forward and focus on other priorities.

In my life today, I spend less time thinking about what could have been, and instead choose to keep my eyes focused on what is ahead. As Mr. Lynn always said, "Never let your current obstacles dampen the brightness of your future." I am eternally grateful to Mr. Lynn and the pivotal role he played in my life. The takeaway lesson should be clear: It is not how many times you get knocked down that defines your character and legacy; instead, it is how you respond that will determine your forward progress. Sometimes in life, setbacks will serve as a setup for something better!

Chapter 5

Crash Course on Adulthood and Family Responsibilities

"There are stark differences we experience in our life as we transition from childhood to adulthood. This journey is filled with many milestones and memories."
– Unknown

URING MY CHILDHOOD in Jane and Finch, I felt like an adult, especially following my parents' separation. The self-imposed pressure to step up and assist my mother had me feeling like a man long before I was ready to become one. In my final year of high school, my mother reminded me of a conversation we had following the departure of my father. We did not talk much about him after he left, so this conversation took me by surprise. She recounted being in the kitchen when I approached her and said in my youthful voice, "Mom, don't worry that Dad has left. I promise I will take care of you."

I could barely take care of myself much less be able to take care of my mother. With university around the corner, I had a lot to learn about adulthood and the responsibilities that came with that transition.

Up to that point, much of what I needed was still provided by my mother, even though I managed to work part-time while in school. I did not fully appreciate what the real world looked like. Ready or not, I was headed for a crash course.

Still glowing from the influence and encouragement from my Grade 11 law teacher, I decided that after high school I wanted to pursue my dream of becoming a lawyer. I applied to multiple programs and was grateful to be accepted to the University of Windsor to study in the Honours Criminology program.

My acceptance was further confirmation that I was on the right track. Many students at the age of eighteen who enter university or college are uncertain about exactly what they want to do and hope to figure it out as they go along. My scenario was different, I had a teacher who helped to narrow my focus, and from that point on, my plan was put into action.

Getting into university was significant on many levels. My immigrant family had left everything behind in Jamaica in search of better opportunities in Canada. Their own dreams were largely replaced with the goal of seeing their children achieve success. It was incumbent on me to prove that their sacrifice had not been wasted. Secondly, a young Black male from the Jane and Finch community having a legitimate shot in becoming a lawyer would be a significant accomplishment. The socioeconomic gaps, poor educational resources, biases, stereotypes, and systemic barriers sealed the fate of many in the community. Failure was not an option; I wanted, and needed, a better outcome.

I was eighteen years old when I entered my first year at the University of Windsor. I was excited for the freedom of being away from home for the first time, but the adjustment was harder than I had imagined. I was hundreds of kilometres away from home when it suddenly dawned on me how much I relied on my family for my necessities and emotional support. At home, my meals were always prepared. I had clean and neatly folded laundry every time I looked in the closet. Even with my part-time job, my mother still provided me with a small allowance that allowed me to splurge on my favourite comic books and other delights. I was officially leaving the comforts of home behind to become independent and pursue my dreams.

I remember my brother Lenny drove me from Toronto to Windsor in his black hatchback, with all my belongings packed tightly in the back. It was not much, but it was mine. We got to my dorm and spent the rest of the afternoon setting up my room. The space itself was the nineties version of the current hit show "Tiny Homes." I had to make a significant adjustment in sharing half of the room with an absolute stranger. I likely could have secured a larger and cheaper space off campus, but I opted for the convenience that on-campus living provided. When my brother drove away that evening, I felt alone, not sure of what I was going to do on my own. Later that evening, the dorm room door opened, only to see a short and stocky Caucasian male enter the room. The moment we locked eyes, we both smiled at each other to acknowledge our odd pairing. I would later learn his name was James Shay from Chatham-Kent, Ontario. While living in Jane and Finch, I was used to having friends from around the world. Therefore, James's presence was far from awkward. Despite our obvious differences, we shared pursuing a career in the legal profession in common. I wanted to be a lawyer, and James had dreams of becoming a police officer. In a matter of days, we formed a bond that was smooth and easy. We were ebony and ivory, destined to live in perfect harmony. The more we learned about each other, the closer we became. He was my brother from another mother, a feeling we mutually shared. While his presence and friendship were certainly welcomed, I still had a lot to figure out, being freshly removed from the comforts of home.

After the first two weeks living on my own, it appeared I had figured out how to live without my family's safety net. I started to believe that

I was wrong about how difficult life would be. I would attend class and come home, and my meals would be waiting for me just to reheat. Reality kicked in after my mom's packed snacks, frozen meals, and clean and folded laundry withered away. It did not take long for me feel like a humpback whale stuck and alone on a sandy beach. I was completely out of my element.

It was a lot harder to simply focus on my studies when I had to shop and prepare my own meals. Moreover, the little money I had saved prior to coming to university was beginning to run out. Instead of waiting for selected groceries to go on sale, I foolishly decided to purchase everything at the regular price. If I continued at that rate, I would be penniless and back at home before the first semester ended.

I was fortunate that my thinning budget got a boost with the receipt of OSAP—Ontario Student Assistant Program—a combination of loans and grants from both the federal and provincial government. The loan covered most of my needs, including tuition, books, and living accommodations. I was convinced that the money was God-sent. Without it, my family could never afford to pay for my education. The money was significant, and I was grateful for it. However, it also meant I had to show a level of maturity and responsibility when it came to managing my funds. I would now have to make financial decisions I never had to make prior to attending university. It was clear when the money was issued that it was not a charitable gift. Therefore, it was shocking to hear stories circulating of students treating their OSAP like an accessible trust fund. Some students used the money to purchase expensive clothing and even cars. We were students, not rockstars. I guess this was part of the learning experience in becoming an independent and responsible adult.

Despite the financial lifeline given in the form of OSAP, I continued to struggle immensely for the first few months. I was constantly on the phone, asking my mother the simplest questions. "How do I cook the rice?" "How do I know when the chicken is cooked?" "Can I mix coloured clothes with white clothes when doing laundry?" These were tasks I had never had to consider while living at home. As the youngest in the family, I got away with doing very little. But I was not in Toronto anymore. I was in Windsor, and the absence of such privileges was a reality check. Now on my own, I was responsible for making my bed, ensuring my room was clean, washing my dishes, removing old food from the fridge, ironing my clothes, and everything else required of someone living independently. Initially, my adjustment was difficult; however, as time went on, I began to figure things out and develop a routine that made me feel more comfortable.

Managing my finances and taking care of my household needs was only part of the equation. I also had to learn to adjust in the classroom. Back in high school, I could get away with studying the night before an exam and still pull off a good grade. As a student at C.W. Jefferys, if I did not show up to class, I could expect a call to my home to check that I was okay. If I failed to perform as expected, it was certain that one of my teachers would pull me aside and give me a pep talk. This level of over-sight would end the moment I stepped foot onto the Windsor campus.

On the first day of classes, all students were told that it was their decision whether they attended classes or not. It was our responsibility to develop the time management skills and study habits needed to succeed in the program. I recall one of my professors saying, "You are all adults, and you will be treated as such." To be honest, I was scared, as this was in sharp contrast to the coddling experience of high school. As much as I wanted to return to my youthful lifestyle, free of responsibilities, there was no turning back. Far from being totally prepared, I was now receiving a crash course on what it meant to be an independent adult.

To alleviate the stresses of being a first-year student, I turned to my familiar love—basketball. Every spare moment, I would head over to the sports facility to practice my dribbling and shooting. I practiced as hard as I played, so each workout allowed me to stay physically fit. I was always at peace on the basketball court. I had played long enough over the years to develop a level of comfort. I often knew what to expect from myself and the competition. It was the lack of predictability that made my transition from high school to university so difficult.

Wanting to carry on the tradition of playing team basketball, I was eager to try out for the varsity team once the opportunity arose. I was not one of the lucky ones to receive a basketball scholarship out of high school, but I was confident in my abilities and the chance of making the team. If selected, I knew basketball would provide the structure and discipline I needed as a freshman on campus. Over the years, my coaches would say, "Team basketball is a reflection of life; it prepares you to be disciplined and to manage your time. It teaches you how to work effectively with others around you." That message did not resonate then as much as it did now.

The moment had officially come. I already had a lot on my plate trying to balance living on my own along with meeting academic expectations at the university level. However, for the first time in my life, I felt like I needed basketball rather than simply playing it for fun. From the first few practices, it was clear that the competition was beyond anything I had previously encountered. Many of us were battling for only a few spots, because the team had several returning players.

After three days of intense practices, I was excited to learn that I had done enough to make the team. I did not have the privileges associated with being a high recruit; I was the classic underdog. My success at the varsity level proved what I could achieve if given the opportunity to show my capabilities. What I did not have in name recognition, I made up with my work ethic, and this would prove to be the winning recipe I could rely on for future success. For now, I was just delighted to officially be a Windsor Lancer. I bonded quickly with the other freshman on the team around our common love for the game and our respective challenges with our newfound independence. It was nice to know that I was not the only one challenged by the transition into adulthood. Everything was slowly coming together. Things were becoming more predictable in my life and that provided a great sense of ease and comfort. Unexpectedly, that comfort would be short-lived, as I was headed for another crash course on how to be responsible for others.

Taking on New Responsibilities

With much focus on my grades, basketball, and friends, I did not have time for much else. My circle of friends was small and limited mostly to members of the basketball team and those I had met in class. Outside of my tight schedule, I would find time to go to the University Centre Cafeteria to grab lunch and the occasional dinner. I was a creature of habit, typically ordering beef lasagna or chicken nuggets and fries.

One afternoon, I was standing in line to get one of my usual meals when I happened to get a glimpse of a woman who caught my attention. I had seen a lot of women since my arrival at Windsor, but none had triggered the feeling I had upon seeing this goddess.

She was a tall, slender, five-feet-eight, beautiful young woman, with flawless brown skin and dark flowing hair. As I stood and watched her, she slowly approached. I turned my head, not wanting to be caught staring. Although not looking, I could feel her presence as her floral scent lingered long enough for me to smell, even after she walked by. Before I could snap out of my trance, she had disappeared without a trace. She had appeared like an angel and evidently left like one. Had I seen where she went, I am not sure I would have had the courage to approach in that moment. I had dated in high school, but by no means was I experienced.

After getting my food, I left the University Centre with a different appetite. If I saw her again, I was determined not to let the opportunity pass to introduce myself. To my disappointment, that moment would not come any time soon. Due to the size of the campus and varied class schedules, you could see a person one day and not see them again for weeks. I was forced to patiently wait for the next chance encounter. In the interim, I thought about her frequently. I repeatedly rehearsed in front of the mirror what I would say if afforded the opportunity. No matter how many times I practiced, I would always get nervous and stumble through my words. I would finally get the chance to meet the woman who occupied my mind for weeks at the highly anticipated first-semester dance party.

I was never much of a dancing and partying type, but I decided to step out of my comfort zone to meet the young woman who had captured my imagination. The evening of the party, I splashed on some Stetson cologne I had picked up at the local Shoppers Drug Mart. On a student budget, that was the best I could do. I put on the best outfit in my closet and made my way to the party. The gathering was held at one of the campus halls. Although very large, every inch of the space was accounted for with young and energetic students. It didn't take long before I ran into some people I recognized and started up a conversation. Not normally the talkative type, I spoke quite a bit to help alleviate my nervousness.

At the right moment, I slipped away from the group, determined to find the one person I had come for. I began walking around the premises to see if I could find her. I did not have to search for long. Through the crowd, I noticed her standing in a corner, talking to someone I did not recognize. I was not exactly sure how I would feel laying eyes on her for a second time after such a long delay. However, seeing that beautiful smile removed any seed of doubt. She seemed immersed in her conversation, not noticing that I was looking directly at her. I took the opportunity to rehearse the opening lines I had practiced for weeks once more.

My body began reacting. I started sweating, and it felt as though a million butterflies had entered my stomach. It was hard to comprehend; I was feeling super-nervous and vulnerable. How could this happen? I had done such a good job at concealing my emotions in the past. I was not supposed to feel this way. Before I could make any sense of what I was going through, I noticed the person she was with had walked away. The moment was finally here. It was now time to approach. I was careful to hide my nervousness while not sounding rehearsed. I was trying my best not to look like a fool.

I introduced myself, forgetting everything I had spent weeks rehearsing. Thankfully, it did not matter, as we spoke for over an hour, completely engaged and enjoying each other's company. I could not help but think that she looked more beautiful up close than from afar. During our conversation, I learned the name of the angel I had seen weeks prior in the student cafeteria. Her name was Sheri-Anne Browne. As we continued to converse, I learned she had two older siblings and was born in St. Vincent, a small island located between St. Lucia and Grenada. She was deeply rooted in her Caribbean culture and was not shy about expressing her values and beliefs. She was ambitious and focused on accomplishing her goals. Her intelligence, beauty, and our shared values had me wanting more.

Our connection was instant, and I longed to see her more following the party. Initially, that was not meant to be, since our respective schedules would present a stumbling block. Over time, we would learn to be more creative in carving out the time to spend together. During the week, we enjoyed walks between classes and met for lunch and dinner at the cafeteria. On the weekends, we would meet at the library on campus to study. It was hardly the romantic encounters that we had hoped for, but we were happy just to share time together.

It was helpful that we spoke on the phone every evening. Conversations would last well into the evening, with a flow and ease expected from couples in a long-term relationship. This routine continued for the remainder of the year, and it became more intense during the summer break while both back in Toronto.

Before meeting Sheri-Anne, I did not think I would have the time to entertain a serious relationship. I was busy with school and basketball. I did not believe that I had the room and time for anything else. For a moment, I questioned whether my budding relationship with her would distract me from my other two loves. Although legitimate questions, I knew her involvement in my life would only add value by making me a better person. Whatever the risks, I was prepared to take them.

Sheri-Anne and I were having a great time together. However, I was protective of my emotions, considering the emotional rollercoaster I went on with my father. The emotional trauma was something I never felt comfortable discussing with anyone. Yes, I had moved on from that experience, but it resulted in my erecting towering walls around my heart. I was hopeful that she knew how I felt about her based on my actions, since I was not any good at communicating my feelings. Gradually, I became more comfortable with being vulnerable, learning what it meant to be in a relationship. For the longest time, I was solely focused on my feelings. With Sheri-Anne, things were different. I was mindful to consider her wants, needs, and aspirations—all the traits of a supportive partner. Our relationship was smooth, as we enjoyed what is typically known as the honeymoon phase. Each day felt like walking into a thrift shop; we were discovering hidden treasures about each other.

We were now entering our second year at the University of Windsor, excited about the student experience and the progression of our relationship. Despite our hectic schedules, we continued to find ways to spend meaningful time together. We were closer than ever before, with both of us now entertaining the thought of what life would look like together in the long term. It was during this phase of developing a deeper connection on an emotional and physical level that I was given the news that changed everything.

It was a Saturday evening that Sheri-Anne had invited me over for dinner. We were accustomed to spending time together and having meals on the weekends, so nothing seemed out of the ordinary. She prepared my favourite dish—spaghetti and meat sauce—which took me no time to devour. I was preparing to sit down to watch T.V. when Sheri-Anne suggested we go for a walk. Thinking nothing of it, we grabbed our jackets and shoes and headed outside. We were barely out for ten minutes, when she stopped suddenly and stared directly at me. Not knowing what was coming, I smiled as I said, "Why do you look so serious?"

She gently grabbed my hand and said, "Steve, I am pregnant."

I hugged her and could only repeat that everything was going to be okay. Truthfully, I was stunned, excited, and scared all at once. I was only nineteen years old. Even though I was six-feet-three and looked mature beyond my years, I was still a child in many ways, learning the ropes of becoming an independent adult.

We both stood in silence, staring into each other's eyes, contemplating the present and future ahead. A million questions ran through my mind. Was I ready to become a father at this age? How would I explain this to my family and, more importantly, my mother? Was I able to manage the demands of being a father, a student, and supportive partner? For the next few weeks, my mind was consumed with how I was going to make this all work. I was used to handling pressure, but this was well beyond anything I had to deal with before.

Even though I was young and financially unstable, I was determined to be a great father. Based on our personalities, I knew Sheri-Anne and I would figure things out together. As first-time parents, we did not have a perfect blueprint for how we would raise our child, but she had unwavering confidence in me as I had in her. Even with our positive outlook, I was still quite nervous about our next steps and breaking the news to our loved ones. The uncertainty of how my family would handle the situation kept me up many nights. I knew I had to inform them immediately, but I struggled with the method. I deliberated in my mind a thousand different ways how I was going to share the biggest moment in my life to date. What exactly would I say? Should I write a letter? Would it be better to communicate the news over the phone? How would I respond to their questions and comments? Would my family be disappointed in me?

My anxiety and stress levels were high, but a part of me took comfort in knowing I had a loving and supportive network. I made the decision to deliver the news face-to-face, because it was the respectful thing to do. Sheri-Anne offered to come with me, but I needed to tackle this on my own. I booked a greyhound ticket and spent the entire five-hour ride lost in my own thoughts. I arrived home to find my mother sitting in the living room. She immediately jumped up and wrapped her arms around me. My visit was a surprise, as I had never mentioned I was coming. Typical of my mother, she wanted to know what I wanted to eat and asked if I needed any pocket money for school. Before I could utter a word, she disappeared into the kitchen to whip up a quick meal. I remained in the living room, contemplating when and how I would deliver the news. My mom was so happy to see me that I considered waiting until the next morning to break the news, but ultimately decided against it. I called her from the kitchen and asked her to sit down. For what seemed like an eternity, I stared into space, my lips feeling like they had been sealed with glue. Sensing something was wrong, my mom asked if I was sick.

After pausing, I managed to blurt out, "My girlfriend is pregnant, and we are having a baby."

The following moments were a blur, as I narrated the story as fast as possible. My mom sat still, expressionless, and motionless. There was a feeling of suspense, not knowing what she was thinking. Following a period of awkward silence, she simply said, "I hope you are prepared to be a responsible father." I nodded in agreement, not fully understanding what that meant. My father had left our family when I was young, which left me without a clear blueprint to follow. However, this was not a moment to make excuses or feel sorry for myself.

Noticing how tense I looked, my mom reached over and gave me the warmest hug and said, "Son, I love you and nothing will ever change that. I am here for you and your new family." She proceeded to ask questions about Sheri-Anne and her family, and requested to meet them in due course. I readily agreed, excited for the opportunity to bring our two families together. Emotionally drained, I excused myself and went to my room.

As I laid in bed that night, I contemplated my mother's words about being a responsible father. I did not have any parenting experience, but I was committed never to repeat the actions of my father. I knew the pain I felt following his departure, and I simply could not repeat that. I was going to provide for my family the guidance and support they needed every step of the way.

Over the next few days at home, I shared the news with each member of my family and close friends, one by one. Everyone said the right things; they all agreed to support Sheri-Anne and me in any way they could. I travelled back to Windsor, confident in the journey ahead. Sheri-Anne and I continued to spend as much time together as before, but instead of dinner dates and deciding what movies to watch on the weekend, we were scheduling medical appointments and purchasing all the necessities for the arrival of our baby. Following several specialist appointments, we learned the gender of our child. We were having a baby boy. As the word got out, many of our friends told us how lucky we were to be having a boy as our first child. Believe it or not, Sheri-Anne and I did not have a preference, which surprised many people around us. We were focused on having a successful delivery. With the gender confirmed, it was now time to engage in the exciting process of choosing a name. To be honest, we were initially overwhelmed with all the suggestions we received from family and friends. After much deliberation and prayer, we settled on the name Devante. It was our first child, so we could be excused for taking our time before coming up with a name that would make a newborn son proud.

While we waited for our son to be born, Sheri-Anne took the lead, reading numerous books, researching what to eat, how to exercise, and what signs to look out for while pregnant. She wanted everything to be perfect, and so did I. Along the way, we received no shortage of advice from our respective families on how to prepare for and raise a healthy child. We had no egos during this process. We knew we had a lot to learn, so we asked many questions, especially from the people who already had children.

Between the two of us, we did not have much money. After all, we were just two young university students pursuing our careers. We were fortunate to have the assistance from loved ones that would make the arrival of our son easier. Following the announcement of the pregnancy, it felt as if everything was happening at warp speed. Life as we once knew it was changing with each passing day. As Sheri-Anne's pregnancy progressed, we made it a point to pause and enjoy the intimate moments of seeing our baby grow—from Sheri-Anne singing to our son to seeing him toss and turn in her stomach. When it came to making her comfortable through the process, I was very supportive, even if it meant donning my clothes in the middle of the night to satisfy random requests for ice cream, sweet pickles, and the occasional Wendy's hamburger. I would do anything to make her and our little boy happy. When I had a moment to reflect alone, the whole experience seemed

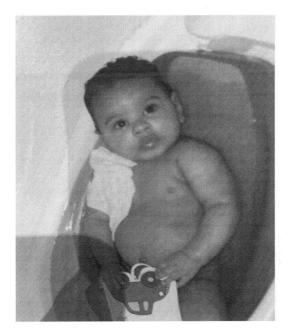

Figure 5.1: A picture of our son Devante

so surreal. It felt like it was only yesterday that we were figuring out ourselves and our relationship, and now we were planning for the arrival of a baby.

We were prepared as well as we could be when our bundle of joy declared he was ready to enter the world. It was after Sheri-Anne's labour contractions began and a few shouts from the nurses to push that our son was born. We were officially parents to a healthy baby boy. There were tears of joy and celebration from family and friends. Amongst the crowd, Sheri-Anne and I locked eyes for a moment, and without saying a word, we both knew our lives had changed instantly for the better.

We both made several difficult decisions and sacrifices to make life comfortable for our son. Splurging on new clothes for ourselves and other frivolous spending was now out of the question. Although we

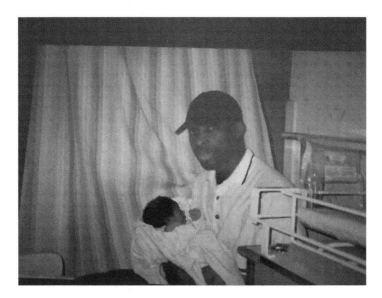

Figure 5.2: At the hospital holding my daughter, Asia

were prepared to sacrifice our personal wants, dropping out of school was never on the table. We both valued education strongly, and with the support of our families and friends, we made it work.

One year later, we had a second child, a precious girl we named Asia. Having a daughter made our young family complete. When Sheri-Anne and I both met, we never could have anticipated having children before finishing university. Having one child in university would have derailed the pursuit of education for many, yet here we were with two young children. Our every movement, inside and outside of the house, had to be planned, deliberated, and executed with precision, with our children at the centre of it all. It was a rollercoaster journey, but we were driven to succeed, personally and for our young family.

Sheri-Anne and I had come a long way after having two children while in university. Through pure grit and determination, we were able to graduate and secure our respective degrees. It was very rewarding to walk onto the graduation stage and receive our diplomas, knowing what

Figure 5.3: Asia and Devante

we had to do to get them. Although very young, our children would witness firsthand how much we valued education.

Looking back, we would not change a single thing. Both our children were as much a source of joy then as they are to us now. For any parent, one of the greatest joys is to see your children pursue and accomplish their dreams. Fast forward to today, our son, Devante, a star athlete after graduating high school, went on to attend the University of Toronto, playing both varsity basketball and soccer. Currently, he is the co-founder and CEO of a revolutionary business called PSLY, found on Google Play and in the Apple Store. Their technology is changing the way people interact with music in social and corporate environments. Within a few months of their official launch, they captured the attention of the music industry and media outlets, with features in Blog TO and Red Bull Innovation.

Our daughter, Asia, completed high school as an Ontario Scholar and attended the University of Toronto, where she graduated with

Figure 5.4: Devante and me at Asia's graduation

an Honours Bachelor of Arts Degree. She is currently a first-year law student attending the Ryerson Faculty of Law Program located in Toronto.

Sadly, in life, not every story has the desired fairy-tale ending. A year after celebrating some of the biggest moments in our lives, including the birth of our two children and completing university, our dreams of growing old together slowly started to disappear. The everyday grind of parenthood took a toll on our relationship. We both still cared deeply for one another, but it was clear that something had changed.

It was not a single event that led to our breakup. Instead, it was the realization that we had grown apart. It was shocking to our friends and family, as we were perceived in their eyes to be a great couple. I believe we were just as shocked by the outcome, since we had never envisioned separation in our plans. Following the birth of our children, we focused all our energy on them, leaving little time to nurture and further develop our relationship. Even with much needed support, it was difficult to have the quality time we needed. Movie dates and long walks in the park were replaced with diaper changes and scrambling to the store for baby formula. We said all the right things about igniting our relationship, and we tried, but deep down inside we both knew that the relationship had run its course.

For a period, I carried the guilt of failing Sheri-Anne and our young family. I had dreamt of marriage, the white picket fence, and house for all of us. However, I was forced to accept the hard truth that things do not always work out as planned, even with the best of intentions. As we grow older, we eventually learn that life is far from perfect and more like a wild ride of pain, disappointment, excitement, and love. Somehow, we must learn to buckle up and enjoy the journey. Although separated, we continued to have tremendous respect and support for each other. After all, we shared a bond that would never be broken. We were committed to being the best parents possible, regardless of the change in our circumstances.

My early twenties provided some pivotal moments, allowing me to understand what it meant to be a responsible adult. Not only was I learning to become self-sufficient, but I was also getting a crash course on being a father and supportive partner. There is a saying that it takes a village to raise a child. That was certainly true in my case. I was challenged every step of the way, but the support from everyone in our inner circle saw me through. As I look back at my time at the University of Windsor, I realize that my life was full of unexpected twists and turns. If I were to draw my life out on a map, there would be several zig zags across the page. For many of us, life rarely offers a straight path to our destination. Through it all, I knew it was important to stay the course. My experiences up to this point taught me an invaluable lesson: Never allow yourself to be defined by your adversities but rather by how you respond to them.

With a Bachelor of Arts Degree (Honours Criminology) now firmly under my belt and two children to take care of, I was more determined than ever to reach my goal of becoming a lawyer. Up next was my application to law school. Although excited about the journey, I would soon encounter another bump in the road that would test my mental fortitude, character, and drive to succeed.

Chapter 6

Law School, the
Unconventional Way

*"Sometimes the road of life takes an unexpected turn, and you have no
choice but to follow it to end up in the place you are supposed to be."*
– Unknown

M Y LIFE AT this point could be best described as challenging. Ian
would always say, "What doesn't kill you will make you stronger."
He was right. I certainly felt stronger, having overcome many of my
challenges and feeling a sense of accomplishment. However, at this
point in my life, I was looking forward to encountering a smoother path
and avoiding the sudden twists and turns. I was enjoying fatherhood
and the fact that I had just recently graduated from the University of
Windsor. I was now focused on applying and getting into law school.

I had everything mapped out. The plan was to attend one of the two
law schools located in the Toronto area. I had considered attending the
University of Windsor, as I had truly enjoyed my time there, but I wanted
to be back home. Sheri-Anne and I had moved back to Toronto following
our graduation to be closer to our support system. With two young

children and the both of us embarking on the next stage of our career paths, we welcomed any assistance we could get from family and friends.

Notwithstanding that nothing in my life up to this point had come easy, I was still very optimistic about my chances of getting into law school. Acceptance into the program would further validate my hard work and the bold prediction of my Grade 11 law teacher. Unfortunately for every dreamer, there are individuals eager to crush them. For some, it was clear that there was only one path for me to take. My friends reported hearing from those familiar with my situation that I should put further schooling behind me. The consensus was that I needed to focus on raising and financially supporting my children with a full-time job.

It was not long before I started hearing the chatter firsthand. I was studying for my law school entry examination (LSAT) at the library at York University when I saw some individuals I recognized from my time back at the University of Windsor. As I approached them from behind, I was surprised to hear my name mentioned in their conversation. Not wanting to be detected, I slipped behind a bookshelf to hear the rest of what was being said. A member of the group confidently declared, "Any hopes of him attending law school is finished with two young kids. What is he thinking?" I felt I was peering into a courtroom, watching my own trial. The jury heard the evidence, briefly deliberated, and rendered a verdict of guilty for trying to pursue my chosen career path. Shocked and hurt, I walked away without confronting them. What would be the point? It was evident that all minds were made up. No longer in the mood to study, I went home.

Although known for projecting a strong exterior, I would be lying if I said that what I overheard did not penetrate me like a knife. I was left to feel that I was choosing my career over my children. After my father walked out on our family for reasons unknown, I had vowed never to choose any person or thing over my own family. Painfully, it felt like history was repeating itself. I spent many nights after school, sitting alone in my room for hours as I pondered the validity of everything being said about me. The more I heard the whispers, the more I felt it was time to walk away from the hopes of becoming a lawyer one day. The whole situation was getting to me, I was officially at a crossroad.

In my moment of indecision, there was a persistent voice commanding me to push forward. The more I questioned myself, the louder the voice became. After calming my emotions, I considered both the short- and long-term implications of my available choices. If I decided against law school and failed to secure more than an entry-level position to support my children, I could only imagine how much more difficult life would be. I had always been resilient, but deep down this was not the path I wanted to take. On the other hand, If I pursued a career in law, the journey would be strenuous, but it would be fulfilling and would allow me to care for my children in the way I had always imagined. Most parents want to expose their children to an array of opportunities, while helping them to become financially stable. I was determined to do the same for my children.

Still looking for an outward sign to reinforce my decision, I reflected on how my mother relied on her faith to handle challenges and provide direction for the difficult decisions she had to make. I was far from being the little boy she took to church service every Saturday morning, but I still believed in the value of church and would attend whenever time permitted. It dawned on me that this was the place I needed to be. The following weekend, I attended service, looking for confirmation, and I was not disappointed. Midway into the sermon, I heard the pastor say, "If your path is more difficult, it is because of your high calling." That was it! Even with hundreds of people at church that morning, I knew he was speaking directly to me and my situation. His words had just summed up my journey up to that point. The challenges in my life would lead me to something greater. Some may argue that his words that morning were merely coincidental, but I was used to getting a word of inspiration in this environment when I needed it most. The pastor's message that morning was another example of God showing me the way. I left the church feeling confident in the path I needed to take.

I was very fortunate that my decision to apply to law school was supported by the mother of my children, Sheri-Anne, my family, and my close friends. A decision of this magnitude could not have been easily made on my own. I was coparenting, so it was important that I first discussed my immediate plans with Sheri-Anne to achieve harmony. We respected each other enough to have those important discussions.

I cannot overstate the support and sacrifices Sheri-Anne continued to make for our family after moving back to Toronto. She quickly secured an apartment, making sure that the children were comfortable. We were fortunate to receive childcare assistance, which allowed her to work full-time. Her employment meant that the needs of our children would always be met. However, the rush to secure a steady income resulted in her career ambitions being placed on hold. Although I was a very involved father and worked part-time to contribute, it was clear that she was the primary provider for our young children. Admittedly, I could have done more if I had put law school on the back burner. I was confident she was hearing from individuals who expressed similar thoughts, but she never placed any pressure on me. Ultimately, Sheri-Anne was confident that my decision to pursue my legal studies would benefit our children in the long run. I will never forget her patience and understanding.

I was also blessed with great friends, like Andrew Guy, who was always willing and able to lend a hand of support. Among my friends, he was the first to purchase a car, which he did not hesitate to use to help those in need. If I asked him for a ride to pick up the children, to take them shopping or to medical appointments, he was always there. Often willing to put the others' best interest before himself, I knew I could rely on him if I had to attend law school outside of Toronto. I had peace of mind knowing that he would step in to help Sheri-Anne and the children whenever needed.

My mother and the rest of my family were my greatest support system. They all jumped in from the very beginning to provide emotional and financial assistance. I was blessed to have a large and loving family that cared and supported me through all my challenges. I knew if I got accepted into law school, I would need to lean on my support system more than ever before. I was always grateful for the help I received, but I was mindful never to abuse the willingness of those who were prepared to make sacrifices on my behalf. The children were my responsibility, but I welcomed the assistance.

The unconditional support from everyone around me lifted a huge weight off my shoulders and allowed me to pursue my career path without the burden of guilt and worry. Even with a solid network of support, I would not be shielded from the challenges and obstacles waiting ahead. I was fortunate to have my best friend, Ian, who was also applying for law school, to share the experience with. Ian and I were not the sentimental types, so we never formally sat down to discuss how we would feel if we both got accepted into law school. From the moment we decided to submit our applications, it was strictly business. We were both raised in the Jane and Finch community and both products of single-parent households. We shared similar experiences with our fathers growing up, so we were quite good at showing a strong exterior while masking our true emotions. Quite frankly, there was no need to verbalize the moment. We both knew what was at stake, considering the barrier of low expectations placed on our community due to its reputation of drugs, gangs, and violence.

Two Black males emerging from humble beginnings, taking on the world, and becoming successful lawyers would provide a lasting example of what is possible for youths in our community.

Focused on our goals, we spent weeks researching every law school in North America. Initially, I had only considered attending one of the two law schools in Toronto. However, after speaking with Ian, it became clear that I needed to expand my opportunities. With the law school application process being very competitive, this decision made sense. We made a list of the positives and negatives of each university, the admission requirements, the reputation of the institution, and the percentage of those who graduated and immediately secured jobs. We discussed attending the most prestigious schools, but we were always cognizant of our financial realities. As a result, we sent out dozens of applications to schools throughout Canada and the United States with the hopes of hearing from at least one. We both agreed to open our notice letters together as a show of solidarity and support.

The first few application responses were not what we had hoped. They all had the standard line, "Thank you for applying, but we regret to inform you that your application has not been accepted." Despite the early rejections, we both remained hopeful that something positive was just around the corner. The wait was excruciating. There was nothing else we could do after submitting our applications. A group of strangers sitting on an Admission Committee would ultimately decide our fate. We both knew we were up against strong competition from very bright students across the country, also seeking to obtain the few coveted spots. Each year, there was always more student applications compared to the spots available. Applying and getting accepted into law school felt like playing and winning the lottery.

Young, Black, and determined, Ian and I were never ones to back down from a challenge, no matter how difficult. After many sleepless nights and anxious moments, a lifeline was extended from an unexpected source. I got accepted to the University of Detroit Mercy Law School and Ian to the University of Manitoba. My acceptance was confirmation of my abilities and proof that all the sacrifices made to get me to this point were not in vain. The pressure of getting into a law school was now lifted off my shoulders, but this was just one step of the many that remained.

Once the jubilee of my acceptance dissipated, I was forced to face the costs associated with my decision to attend law school in the United States. The Ontario Student Assistant Program (OSAP) provided a maximum of $5,000 CAD, nowhere near the $20,000 USD required for my first-year tuition at the University of Detroit Mercy. Once again, I was facing what appeared to be an insurmountable challenge. I was used to controlling my pathway through hard work. However, this had nothing to do with effort; it was purely financial. I was feeling helpless. I was from a single-parent household, where my mother worked in a paper factory. We were not wealthy by any means.

Over the next few days, I was withdrawn from my family, choosing to spend most of the time in my room. I felt everything I had worked so hard for was slipping away. After sensing I was not acting normally, my mother decided to take matters into her own hands. One evening after dinner, she opened my bedroom door and said, "Steve, I know things don't look good right now, but you must believe." She was right; my faith should have been stronger, considering that it was God that I had turned to when I needed guidance in applying to law school. I immediately proceeded to the living room and picked up the one book often used by my family to provide solutions in moments like this—the Bible. Although I attended church, I did not read the Bible daily. Finding answers when they were needed worked for the rest of my family, so I decided to give it a shot.

As I randomly scrolled through the pages, I landed on Philippians 4:6-7, which says, *"Do not be anxious about anything, but in every situation, by prayer and petition with thanksgiving, present your requests to God and the peace of God, which transcends all understanding, will guard your hearts and your minds in Christ Jesus."* I put down the Bible, feeling confident but still unsure of how my financial predicament would be resolved. However, God had seen it fit to take me this far, and He would continue to open doors that appeared closed. In short order, the idea came to me that I should inform the school of my financial situation.

After some back and forth, I was able to start classes without having my tuition paid in full. I was extremely grateful, but I entered my first semester without a clear plan of how to pay the $20,000 USD tuition fee. I applied for as many jobs as I could, but my options were limited since I was not a U.S. resident. Three weeks into the semester, my prayers were answered when I was offered employment at the main administration office on campus. With my employment earnings, loan from OSAP, and help received from my family, I was able to pay my tuition for the year. More than ever before, I was convinced that no matter what obstacle came my way, I was going to overcome it.

The first few months were a blur between classes, studying for my courses, working, and finding time for my two young children. To the surprise of some of my peers, I still managed to find the time and energy to run for the role of class vice-president on the promise of being a reliable and strong advocate for all first-year students. Thinking back, I really surprised myself. I was a Canadian in a foreign country, with a bold vision of leading a class of American law students. I was completely out of my element but entered the race with confidence. After a hard-fought and gruelling two weeks, I was elected to the position, beating out two very qualified candidates. This was officially my first taste of running a mini-political campaign, which included articulating a vision and securing votes. Little did I know that this would come into play in the future.

With the highly competitive G. Mennen Williams Moot Competition only two weeks after the elections, I would get the opportunity to further test my advocacy skills. The event would be judged by well-established lawyers in the community. Unlike some of my classmates,

I took this competition very seriously. As far as I was concerned, my budding legal reputation was on the line. Among my circle of friends, I was well-known for my competitive nature, so I took on this challenge with the expectation to win. In my mind, it was important to show everyone what this young Black man from Jane and Finch could do. Call it crazy, but I felt the need to defend my reputation and that of the community in every space I entered. After years of living in a neighbourhood labelled with consistent negativity, I was a man on a mission to prove the naysayers wrong. It was me against the world.

As it turned out, I did not win, but I was fortunate to advance to the quarter final round, getting great feedback and a framed certificate for my efforts. I was doing well socially and academically. I scored a 4.0 GPA, finishing at the top of my criminal law class. My hard work led to a nomination for the prestigious Cali Book Award. My performance that year was proof that I belonged. I was proud of myself for what I had accomplished in my first year, but I knew I had to make a radical change. The financial burden was too much to handle. I needed to find a way to reduce the pressure I was under.

Time to Re-group

After careful consideration, I made the difficult decision to take a year off to address my financial situation. This was one of the hardest decisions I had ever had to make. I was doing well, had made some good friends, and was now leaving it all behind. Although disappointed, I was determined to make my way back to school the following year. Having no time to waste, I quickly found a job as a collections officer. I was surprised when I was given the responsibility to call students who had defaulted on their loans.

I felt conflicted making these calls. A part of me was angry that there were those who were privileged to receive funding to pursue their education and yet refused to pay it back. On the other hand, I knew firsthand the many struggles that students face. Ultimately, I could not help but to feel sympathetic about their predicaments. With a few bad bounces, I could've easily been one of the students at the other end of my calls. With no other employment options at the time, I had to put my personal feelings aside. I felt fortunate to financially provide for my children while diligently saving as much as I could. It was important to pay for my tuition without relying on friends and family this time around.

Working the entire summer allowed me to save the necessary funds, but this was only a short-term solution. The thought of taking every other year off to work and save for my tuition was not ideal. Life was just handing me one challenge after another. I was having to remove mountains just to take one step forward. At this point in my life, I knew feeling sorry for myself would not get me further ahead. It was time to come up with another plan, but I was not sure where to begin.

A Change in Direction

I was preparing to register for my second year of law school, when I decided to look for bursaries and scholarships to help offset my expenses. I was browsing through the University of Detroit Mercy scholarship and bursaries page, when my eyes were drawn to the heading "Study at Another Institution in the United States or Internationally." I concluded this was new, since I had not seen this before on previous searches. Curious, I continued to scroll down the page, looking for further details. At the time, it did not occur to me that what I was looking at was information that would change the trajectory of my studies and provide a solution to the financial dilemma.

The criteria appeared straightforward. To qualify, students had to meet the stated GPA requirements and get approval from the Dean of Academics. Secondly, your application to study abroad had to be accepted by your school of choice. The process was formally called a Letter of Permission. In essence, it allows a student to study at another school for one year with the understanding that they must return to their home school upon completion, with no exceptions.

As I continued with my research, I learned that this program was popular among students, with only a limited number of applications approved each year. Despite the odds, I was motivated to have the opportunity to return to Canada and study law in the country I was born, even if only for one year. I was also excited to take advantage of the relief in tuition fees. At the time, law school tuition in Ontario ranged from $4,000 to $6,000 dollars annually compared to the $20,000 dollars I had to pay in the US. My ability to study abroad seemed like a long shot, but the potential reward was too good not to make the effort.

As I contemplated my next steps, my best friend, Ian, came to mind. If I was going to make a pitch to switch schools, I wanted to do it with him. It was our dream as youths growing up in Jane and Finch to potentially attend law school together. Ian was entering his third year at the University of Manitoba when I approached him with the idea. He was immediately in favour of the proposed plan. His quick endorsement gave me the feeling that we were on the verge of something historic. We both understood it would be a long shot getting into the same school; however, we were hopeful that something magical would happen. After some back and forth, we decided to apply to the University of Ottawa, Faculty of Law Program. Thinking back, I am not sure why, out of all the Canadian universities, we chose Ottawa. It was not close to home, nor did we know anyone who was currently attending, or had formerly attended, the school. Whatever the reasons at the time, it proved to be the best decision for me.

Like our law school applications a few years back, each day we checked the mail, eager for a response. This time was slightly different, because we decided to let our guards down, openly discussing our feelings of attending law school together. Knowing Ian, it would be just like old times when we attended the same high school. Lightning had already struck once with the both of us getting accepted into law school. As each day passed, we wondered if lightning would strike twice, allowing us to join forces in Ottawa. We were both growing impatient with waiting, and it was hard to focus on anything else. Then it happened.

The day started like most, with me going to the mailbox first thing after work. I opened the box, expecting to see the usual flyers, bills, and other junk mail, but something immediately caught my attention. I saw the logo and seal of the University of Ottawa on the outside of one of the envelopes. My immediate instinct was to rip the envelope open, as I had been anxiously awaiting its arrival. Instead, I brought the mail in the house and went upstairs to my room without saying a word to anyone. I sat down on my bed and said a prayer. I was suddenly calm and mentally prepared to accept the outcome, whatever it was. My mother always said, "What is meant for you, nobody can take it away from you." I ripped open the envelope, and with the letter in hand, my eyes raced to the bottom of the page. I was searching for one word, and I found it: ACCEPTED!

With the feeling of excitement welling up inside me, all I wanted to do was shout. However, I kept my composure, wanting to hear if Ian had received similar news. Before I could call him, my phone rang, and it was him yelling, "I got in! I got in!"

It was hard to digest that this was happening for the both of us. It felt like a script for a Hollywood movie. Two young men beating the odds to achieve mainstream success. The magnitude of the moment made us appreciate how far we had come. However, there was little time to remain caught up in our feelings, as we had several quick decisions to make.

We immediately sorted out our living arrangements, renting two rooms in a townhouse in the suburbs of Orleans. It would be a thirty-minute bus ride from the main campus and Faculty of Law building. My acceptance to the law program in Ottawa was bittersweet, because, once again, it meant I was going to be away from my children. However, I was confident, more than ever, that the sacrifice would be worth it.

Ian and I immediately immersed ourselves in the Ottawa community, learning as much as we could about our new surroundings. We only had one year in Ottawa, so we had to hit the ground running. I was eager to make new friends and make my presence known. In my first semester, I joined the Black Law Students Association and the Business Law Students Society. As people on campus learned more about Ian, me, and our journey to law school, it began to catch the attention of faculty members. It was not long before we were approached by the head of the Law Faculty's Outreach Team and asked of our willingness to visit local high schools and speak to Grade 12 students about our experiences leading up to law school. The mission was clear: Go and inspire a new and diverse generation to consider law as a career opportunity.

Ian and I had a journey that was different from most, making us prime candidates for the law school's community outreach efforts, especially among visible minorities. Ian would always say that coming from the Jane and Finch community made us special. For many others who lived under constant police surveillance, suspicion based on race, culture, and religion, it was difficult to feel that way. Not Ian. From the first day we met, it was clear that his view of life and sense of value was different from most. He was the eternal optimist, refusing to let his surrounding circumstances define his outcome. Our friendship thrived because we were likeminded and often on the same page. Although we both had busy schedules at the time, we were honoured to be given the platform and readily agreed to assist. Growing up, we both understood the power of positive affirmation and being inspired by others to pursue and achieve success. The thought of doing that for someone else made us both proud.

When I initially arrived in Ottawa, my plan was to get involved, do well academically, and prepare for my return to the University of Detroit Mercy for the next calendar year. It was not long into my first semester that that plan was scrapped for a new one. I was really enjoying my time in Ottawa; it was a feeling and experience I did not want to let go. Furthermore, I could not ignore the obvious. I was financially better off in Ottawa. The thought of returning to Detroit to face the huge financial burden became harder and harder to accept. Mentally, I made the decision to stay, but I did not have a clue how I was going to make that happen.

Once again, I was faced with another major obstacle. For days, I contemplated every angle to pull it off. It suddenly dawned on me that if I was going to do this, I needed to rally the support of my professors. Before doing so, I decided to test the waters by booking an appointment with the Associate Dean to discuss my intention of continuing my studies at the university. I was fortunate that he had an opening to see me the next day. Without a lot of time to prepare, I decided I was going to speak from the heart. I was extremely nervous, as this was my first time speaking to the Associate Dean. I did not know what he would think of my desire to stay rather than return to the University of Detroit Mercy.

I recall arriving at the administration office, and within five minutes, I was escorted directly into his office. It did not take long before he said, "How can I help you?" I could tell he already knew all about me, after seeing my file on his desk. I decided to get right into it and told him that my Letter of Permission to remain at the university was expiring at the end of the year, but I wanted to stay and continue my studies. I laid out all my reasons. He patiently listened with no reaction. As I continued to speak, I could not help but wonder if he was supportive of what I was saying or if he was waiting until I finished to politely tell me to leave. I finished my comments with, "It is my hope that I can transfer and become a full-time student in the Ottawa Faculty of Law program."

Following a dramatic pause, he leaned back into his chair with his arms folded and began staring at the ceiling. It appeared that he was recapping all I had said and deciding how he was going to respond. His moment of thoughtful reflection was technically only a few seconds, but it felt like an eternity. He broke the silence, and any hopes of my staying, with the following words: "Steve, this has never been done before in the history of this school that I am aware of. I am sorry to say, but you must return to Detroit at the end of the year as stipulated in your study abroad agreement." He thanked me for providing positive feedback about the program and wished me well for the rest of the year. I certainly was not expecting such a strong response. I was obviously devastated by what I had heard. Despite the disappointing news, I had a plan, and I was going to see it through to the end.

For the remainder of the first and second semester, I continued to work hard in class, while still finding time to be involved in several social clubs and other on- and off-campus initiatives.

Compared to my time in Detroit, I truly felt relaxed. I was also with my best friend, who could make a Russian interrogator smile with his warm personality. As expected, we were supportive of each other, which added to the ease that I felt. Even with his encouragement, I could not escape the fact that the clock was ticking on my time in Ottawa. I was the male version of Cinderella at the ball, worried that my fairy-tale experience was coming to an unfortunate end.

My blueprint to stay was simple, but not easy to achieve. It meant taking my participation in school to another level. I was committed to working harder, getting better grades, and becoming more involved in school activities. In addition to my efforts, it was also crucial to secure the support of most, if not all, of my professors in my desire to stay.

Time would reveal that I would only need the support of one, whose active campaign would help me accomplish the impossible. That person was none other than Constitutional Law Professor Joanne St. Lewis. I met her on several occasions while attending various on-campus programs and initiatives. For many students, she was more than a professor. After spending only a few moments with her, you felt like a member of her family. Her personal story and stance on social equality and justice resonated with me. We bonded rather quickly, so I felt comfortable sharing my predicament and need for assistance.

Without hesitation Professor Lewis readily agreed to offer her support, and we immediately began to devise a plan with military precision on how we would strike. She was clear from the beginning that success would be difficult, but I had nothing to lose and a world to gain. I left our initial meeting confident that I was in good hands. If Professor Lewis believed in you, she could single-handily move a mountain for you. I was hopeful she could do something for me. I was fortunate to have the support of other professors, but Joanne St. Lewis was my biggest cheerleader by far. She was a well-respected professor, so when she spoke many people listened. Through her advocacy, she did her best to convince the Dean and Associate Dean that I was a student worthy of changing the rules for. It helped my case that I continued to do well academically, but I was not sure if it was going to be enough.

The school year had finished, and I honestly had no clue if I would be staying or returning to Detroit. It was two agonizing weeks before I heard word on my fate. This time, there was no letter. I received an email from the Dean with the subject line, ADMISSION. Scrolling quickly past the introductory remarks, my eyes locked on the words that would change everything: "After careful consideration, it gives me great pleasure to extend an offer of acceptance to attend the University of Ottawa Faculty of Law Program." I read the email several more times to make sure that it was real.

Crying was never my speciality, but in that moment, I allowed myself just to let go. With one email, my life was changed in an instant. No more financial instability and uncertainty. Every step of the way up to that point had been challenging, so it was nice to know that things were going to get easier.

I proceeded to call the one person who had made this possible. I do not remember the details of the call with Professor St. Lewis other than my repeating how grateful I was. I then called my family to share the news. I told Ian of the email when he arrived home later that evening. That night, for the first time, I fell asleep without having to worry about how I was going to make things work. The next morning, it dawned on me that I had made history at the University of Ottawa. It was only a short time ago that the Associate Dean had told me that my request to be accepted following the expiry of my Letter of Permission was not possible. As far as he was concerned, the University had never accepted a student off a Letter of Permission, and I would not be the first. Luckily for me, fate would yield me a different outcome. This history-making accomplishment would have been enough for a lifetime, but I would later embark on several history-making events that would take me by complete surprise.

I was going to miss the many friends I had made in Detroit, but this was the right decision for me and my family. I returned the next year to Ottawa with the weight of the world lifted off my shoulders. With no other major obstacles in the way, I went on to graduate from the University of Ottawa with Second Class Honours. I accumulated many fond memories during my time in Ottawa. However, it was one conversation with fellow Black law students that stuck with me and became a sign of things to come.

We were discussing securing employment following graduation, when the conversation turned to what they were planning to put on their resume and job applications. Some were seriously apprehensive about mentioning that they were members of the Black Law Student Association. The belief was that if the prospective employer knew their race, they would not be afforded an interview. They began to share stories of other students changing their afro-centric names and altering the texture of their hair to be deemed acceptable for employment opportunities. At the time, I did not fully appreciate the concern. After all, we were educated law students, not begging paupers. I was extremely confident that our achievements would open every door we planned on entering. Why would we need to conceal our authentic selves and what we represent? Dismissive of what was said, I arrogantly declared I was not changing anything and would document all social affiliations on my job applications. True to my word, I did and went on to secure a dream job in a place with strong connections to my childhood. I had proven that the concerns were misplaced. There was nothing to worry about. To my surprise, I would soon learn that my educational achievements would not shield me from the concerns my fellow students were forecasting. Sadly, I would also struggle with the hesitancy of inserting my full blackness into predominantly Caucasian spaces.

Chapter 7

Next Stop: The Toronto Transit Commission

"There is nowhere you can be that is not where you are meant to be."
— John Lennon

I HAD JUST graduated from the University of Ottawa Faculty of Law Program with Second Class Honours. I was extremely happy to be back in Toronto. Prior to graduating, I was looking to secure a job otherwise known as an articling position. For those unfamiliar with the term "articling," it is a paid position, generally under the supervision of a senior lawyer, designed to provide professional development and real-life experience in the legal profession. In 2003, the articling period was twelve months. With the successful completion of your articles, bar examinations, and call to the bar, your employer reserved the right to hire you back as a licensed lawyer.

The process was extremely competitive, since there are often more students than available positions. If you were fortunate to land one of these precious opportunities, you were now one step closer to financial stability as a practicing lawyer. Depending on the size of the firm, one could easily earn over $100,000 in the first year of practice. In terms of my job search, I casted my net wide, hoping to find a position that would provide me with litigation experience. In law school, I was fascinated with the various aspects of litigation, so focusing on this area just made sense. I was fortunate to receive several interview requests, including from the Department of Justice Canada, but it was the one from the TTC that really captured my attention. Working for the company where I had such fond memories as a youth would be extra special.

When I interviewed with the TTC Legal Department, it was made clear that the position was for one year, and it was very unlikely that I would be hired back full-time at the end of my term. It was impressed upon me that it had been several years since the Legal Department hired a student following the end of their contract. As consolation, I was told that my experience working for the TTC would make me a competitive candidate when attempting to secure a job with another employer. Fresh from overcoming impossible odds, just to get accepted and graduate from the law program in Ottawa, I was not discouraged by what seemed like a foregone conclusion. My experiences up to that had taught me to expect the unexpected. My primary focus was to earn some much-needed income. I would worry about my future employment prospects at the appropriate time. The articling position paid well, but I was equally attracted to the cool factor of working for one of Canada's most recognizable companies. Everyone in Toronto, in Canada, and around the world was familiar with the TTC brand. Working for this company would certainly give me some bragging rights among my peers.

During the interview process, I learned that the legal department had received over one hundred applications for the one position. Unlike many medium-to-large firms at the time, the TTC only hired one articling student, which resulted in the process being more competitive than usual. I felt the interview went well, as there were a lot of smiles and laughter following my responses. I am generally very comfortable with interviewing, since it affords me the opportunity to showcase my confidence, knowledge, and personality. A few days later, I was called back for a second interview. Feeling more confident, I reviewed my notes from the first interview and headed down to TTC headquarters at 1900 Yonge Street, unsure of what to expect. When I arrived, the scene in the interview room was noticeably different. This time, there were more people in the room, including the Senior Lawyer and the Associate General Counsel. On the table, I noticed my resume in front of each person, with different sections highlighted in yellow. The atmosphere was intimidating, but this was not the time to crumble under the pressure. Following a brief round of introductions, I was peppered with questions ranging from my grades to my work experience and why I was the best candidate for the position.

I answered each question the best I could, but it was difficult to tell if my answers were hitting the mark. As I looked at their blank faces, I could not help but feel as though I was in a room full of professional poker players. Many things were going through my mind, but I had to keep my composure. After an hour or so, it was over. I was told I would learn of the outcome later in the day. I smiled and said "Thank you." I was careful to shake every hand before leaving, wanting to solidify the personal connections I had made in the room.

The second interview was certainly more intense than the first, but I left feeling confident with what I had done. When I got home, I went straight to my room to avoid the inevitable questions about how the interview went. I did not want to falsely raise my family's hopes, just to let them down with the news that I did not get the job. I sat on my bed, still in my interview clothes, thinking about how this opportunity could change my life.

It was around 4:30 PM that afternoon when I received a call from the Associate General Counsel. There was little suspense. Wasting no time, she said, "Steve, congratulations on a successful interview. We want to offer you the job." My voice trembling with excitement, I said, "Yes." Following the conversation, my mind immediately turned to what this meant for my future. The next day, I returned to the legal department to complete some paperwork and was greeted by one of the lawyers who had interviewed me. He proceeded to inform me that my hire came down to a photo finish with a female student to whom they had also granted a second interview. I smiled, knowing that I had done just enough to make the cut. I was highly motivated to show my new employer that they had made the right choice.

Looking back, the whole interview experience, and landing the job, was surreal. As I have already shared in my story, when I was a child growing up in Jane and Finch, I would take the TTC 35 Jane bus with my mother every Saturday morning to attend church services. I vividly recall wanting to be a TTC bus driver, imagining myself wearing the iconic blue shirt, red tie, and grey pants. I was committed to driving the same 35 Jane route from Jane and Steeles to Jane Station. After all, this was the only route I really knew.

As a young passenger on the TTC bus, I depended on the bus drivers to take me safely to my destination. Many years later, bus drivers would now depend on me to represent them in court. Even though I was determined to become a lawyer after receiving a positive endorsement in Grade 11, I never could have imagined working in the TTC's Legal Department. From the start, my articling experience was different from that of many of my peers at the time. The fact that many firms hired a greater number of students meant there was a natural development of camaraderie among the group. The ability to share your thoughts, questions, and concerns with those travelling the same path made the whole process easier to navigate. However, as the lone student hired by the TTC Legal Department, I did not have such a cushion. Not having another student around proved difficult, but I was determined not to use this as an excuse to be less than successful. I was fortunate that the lawyers, claims adjusters, and staff did their best to make my transition smooth.

Over the next twelve months, I worked for several lawyers, performing research, drafting reports, and preparing motion materials. I also managed a small number of files, which included Workers' Criminal Injuries Compensation, Small Claims Court, and Highway Traffic Act matters. With each file, research assignment, and successful result in court, I was earning the trust and respect of my colleagues. I was developing a reputation of one who could be counted on. My hard work was rewarded when I was asked by the Associate General Counsel to assist in a high-profile trial that was garnering media attention. I conducted research, drafted motion materials, and was part of the legal team that attended court every day. It is every student's dream to feel valued and work on something meaningful.

During my articles, I would hear about the dissatisfaction of students at other firms who were bored just doing research assignments. In some instances, students were reduced to picking up coffee and dry cleaning for lawyers in the office. The type of work I was engaged in, and the relationships I was establishing with judges and other legal counsel outside the TTC, gave me a competitive edge over most of my peers. At this point, I was feeling confident in the skills I was developing. If the TTC decided not to hire me back at the end of my contract, I was certain to land on my feet with another company. Truthfully, though, I did not want to go anywhere else. Those who are fortunate to secure full-time employment with the TTC often end up working their entire careers for the organization. Not fully a year in, I could already see why people were reluctant to leave. The benefits, pension, work-life balance, and the people made it a desirable place to be. I did my best not to get emotionally attached or think of my prospects since it was made clear in my initial interview that I would not be hired back.

Instead of focusing on matters out of my control, I decided to learn as much as I could while I had the opportunity. When away from the office, I would reflect on my journey and pinch myself to ensure this was not a dream. I had come a long way and was now doing exactly what I loved. On the other hand, it was painful to know I would never get the opportunity to thank my Grade 11 law teacher for setting my legal path in motion. I wished she could see what I was doing now. I wanted her to know what her words had done for me. As the universe would have it, she had retired a few years prior to my completion of law school. Since I was unable to speak to her, I would honour her by becoming the best lawyer and leader possible.

As the saying goes, "Time flies when you're having fun." With only two months left in my contract and a short time thereafter from my call to the Legal Bar of Ontario, I began looking for a new job. This would be the last step in my journey before starting my career as a licensed lawyer. I had yet to send out a single application when I stumbled upon an unexpected job opening in the TTC Legal Department. It was always my routine at the beginning of my shift to sift through my emails to see if I had received work from any of the lawyers. As I was getting ready to sign out, I saw an internal posting from our department seeking to hire a new lawyer. This came as a complete surprise, as I had heard nothing about anyone wanting to leave. How was this possible? Nobody leaves the TTC once they get in, or so I thought. I soon learned that the person leaving was one of the lawyers who had initially interviewed me and advocated strongly for my hire. He was now departing for a new opportunity. It took a bit of time to wrap my head around the news. In my mind, I was already preparing to leave, and now there was a sliver of hope that I could stay. For those familiar with the Bible, there is a reference to God parting the Red Sea to allow His chosen people to escape fear, doubt, and an uncertain future. The faithful crossing of the Red Sea led to a fresh start. Similarly, for me, the opening of this opportunity represented security and stability, as I was making the transition from a student to a lawyer.

By the afternoon, everyone was talking about the job posting, as the news had travelled quickly throughout the department. I was pleasantly surprised when one of the legal assistants casually placed a hard copy of the posting on my desk, followed only by a smile. I was fortunate to have made a positive impression in the office, so I knew several people would be rooting for me. However, my budding optimism was almost dashed when I read the job description and immediately realized that I was at a disadvantage.

The posting read, "The TTC Legal and Claims Department is looking for a senior lawyer with 8-10 years of litigation experience to join our team." I was an articling student with barely one year of experience. Of course, I thought my chances were slim. Trying to remain positive, I concluded that I had one major advantage over the other candidates, considering that I had worked with the entire team for almost twelve months. By all accounts, I was well-liked by my peers, and they were all familiar with my work ethic. Just like many situations in my life, the odds were stacked high against me, but as usual, I was up for the challenge.

The job posting received a tremendous response from junior to senior lawyers looking to join the TTC Legal Department. I was not surprised by the response, as working for the TTC had its own prestige. The compensation and work-life balance were very attractive, and many in the legal profession took notice. To make matters more nerve-wracking, I was selected as the first person to be interviewed for the position. One of the senior lawyers and the head of the legal department interviewed me. It was quite an awkward experience. I had chatted and joked with the two throughout the day, and suddenly we were now formal and serious. A short time ago, I was interviewing for an article position, and now I was battling for the start of my legal career. The stakes were high. Securing the position would mean everything to me. Although I knew both men conducting the interview, there was not a hint of favouritism, and I expected nothing less. I believe my interview went well, even though both men wore their best poker faces. I left the interview confident but knowing there was plenty of serious competition to follow.

It took a week for the interviews to be completed and another full week before the final decision was made. I was at my desk when the head of the legal department approached and asked that I meet him in his office. He never said why, but my gut was telling me that it was decision day. I gathered myself and grabbed a notepad just in case I was wrong. As I walked to his office, many thoughts raced through my mind. It did not help that the office was unusually quiet that morning. As I reached the front door, I saw him and the senior lawyer who had interviewed me already seated inside. I immediately took a seat and waited for them to speak. While I appeared calm and collected on the outside, on the inside, there was a tidal wave of nerves.

As the men talked among themselves, I reflected on the nearly twelve months working at the TTC and all the good friends I had made. I thought about how life would be if I were hired. Before I could go to the next thought, the Head of the legal department asked several questions about my workload and how I was managing. I responded, "Nothing that I can't handle." Just like that, the small talk was over. The next thing I heard was, "Steve, we have made a decision. We had some really good candidates with an array of experience, but we are excited to offer you the position."

With those words, it was official. I was now a full-time employee with the TTC. This was the biggest moment in my young professional career, but surprisingly my response was muted. There were no tears or hugs, only a simple thank you, followed by a firm handshake. I returned to my cubicle without saying a word to anyone and sat in a daze for the rest of the day, unable to focus on anything related to my work. I reflected on my childhood growing up in Jane and Finch, and how my mother, family, and close friends had encouraged me every step of the way. I thought about my two children, recalling the time spent away from them, the late nights, early mornings, and the many other sacrifices made to get to this point. This hire was for them and for everyone living in the Jane and Finch community. We had made it!

One of my colleagues who heard the news rushed to my cubicle and said, "You just made history. You are the first Black lawyer to be hired by the TTC Legal and Claims Department since they officially opened on March 30, 1954." I was shocked at my historical achievement, never thinking that I would be the first person of colour hired in this position in fifty years. Although exciting, the news brought to the forefront how instead of celebrating my blackness I attempted to conceal it. When I first accepted my articling position, I became a watered-down version of myself in a blink of an eye. To be clear, nobody told me I had to change, but it was something I felt needed to be done. There was no debate or second guessing, it just happened.

The only Black law student in the department, I was determined not to allow my colour to be a factor or distraction. In essence, I wanted to make sure that everyone was comfortable being around me. I never wanted the work environment to change just because I was around. I was certain if I caused the slightest alteration, my presence would have been resented by some. The goal was to be more like the group, choosing not to reveal my authentic self. Sadly, I had sanitized my Black identity in exchange for acceptance.

I spoke the way my colleagues expected, dressed per expectations, and laughed at all their jokes without hesitation. My actions yielded great results, as I was readily accepted by the group. I was the person they hoped I would be. I was not the stereotypical image of a Black man as seen on television or on the front page of tabloid newspapers. Over the course of my articling term, I regularly listened as my Caucasian colleagues openly shared their experiences without the fear of being judged. Never wanting to be questioned or potentially ridiculed for the language spoken at home, the food we ate, or the music I listened to, I kept my everyday experiences for friends outside of work who could relate. I was living a double life, going undercover every morning I went into work. The acknowledgement that I was the first Black lawyer ever hired in the legal department changed the way I viewed myself and my role at the TTC. It took this news from my colleague for me to realize the person I had become. I now finally understood the concerns and actions taken by some of the Black students back in Ottawa. I did not leave off my affiliation with Black organizations on my previous job applications, but I did do something far worse: I concealed my identity with disturbing ease. The celebration of the moment gave me permission to reclaim my authenticity. Moving forward, I would own my blackness rather than sell it away at the first opportunity. Where is the satisfaction in gaining the world but losing your soul in the process? If you find it difficult to recognize the person you see in the mirror, then it is time for significant changes. I reflected on a valuable lesson from one of the greatest children's stories of all time, *The Wizard of Oz*. "Stop trying to be the person you think everyone expects you to be, and simply be who you are." Although true, for many of us, it is easier said than done.

My newfound courage did not remove the additional pressure and stress that came with my hire. The first Black lawyer hired in the TTC Legal Department came with a new set of responsibilities. With this large platform, I was mindful of how my actions on the job could directly impact whether another person of colour would be hired in a similar position. I was no longer working for myself and my immediate family. In many respects, I was representing the entire Black community. With every accomplishment earned on the job, I was proving to my non-Black counterparts what we were capable of.

I was confident that I had represented myself well as a student, but it was clear I would have to do it all over again as a licensed lawyer. There was no room for errors or slipups if I wanted to ensure I was not the last person of colour hired. Once again, I was never made to feel from anyone that this would be the outcome, but many people of colour know they do not have a long runway to make mistakes without long-term consequences.

For those who do not understand, this type of pressure weighs on you mentally. The need to be perfect to pave the way for others can be exhausting. Being the first was a blessing; but in other ways, it also felt like a curse.

Proving My Worth While Building My Platform

My historical achievement at the TTC afforded me opportunities and privileges that were the envy of many, but it did not shield me from the realities of life in the first few years of my practice. Despite being a newly minted lawyer working for one of the most recognizable companies in Canada, there were those who could not accept that a Black man held this position. I soon learned the painful lesson that success does not guarantee equality, respect, and fair treatment.

On my first day as a professional lawyer, I inherited the files of a twenty-year personal injury lawyer with minimal experience of my own. I knew the challenge was immense, but not outside my capacity. In the weeks that followed, I spent many late nights and early mornings preparing for my first mediation. This was a big deal, because it was my file, there was a considerable amount of money on the line, and I was taking the lead with no assistance. I had to draft the mediation memo, prepare my client, and have my oral submissions typed and ready. I was excited to test my knowledge after all the hard work I had put in. Having a full understanding of the facts and issues in this case, I was prepared for the expected counter-arguments from opposing counsel. However, I was totally unprepared for the blatant disrespect I would receive upon arrival.

As my client and I approached the mediation room, we saw the plaintiff and his lawyer standing in the doorway. Although I reached the doorway first, both the lawyer and the client looked past me and extended their hands to greet my Caucasian client, assuming he was the lawyer. This was done without the opportunity for formal introductions. At first glance, it was automatically assumed that I could not be the lawyer. Many thoughts and feelings surged through my body as I contemplated how to react. Deciding to maintain my composure, I smiled and firmly announced that I was the lawyer representing the TTC. I walked away without saying another word on the matter, leaving behind me mouths wide open. Over the next few months, I encountered similar situations that were subtle, but the impact on me was substantial.

Following these occurrences, I felt powerless, not wanting to be labeled in my young career as a troublemaker by making a formal complaint. I also felt isolated, feeling that no one at work would truly understand what I was going through, so I kept these instances to myself. I was just starting out in my new role at the TTC, and this was not the time to show that I was not strong enough to handle the rigors of the job. Without a doubt, the lack of representation in the legal profession contributed to the reactions I was receiving. The unwanted stares of curiosity and amazement regarding my presence were hard to ignore. If more Black and racialized lawyers were encouraged to enter the profession and given the opportunity to work in high-profiled positions, our presence would be seen as the norm rather than the anomaly.

Despite being subjected to racial stereotypes and biases, I thrived at work, developing a reputation as a young and capable lawyer. I had come too far to allow anyone to chase me away from my goals.

Although excited about my accomplishments, I was most proud of my commitment to inspire youths outside of work. Like my outreach efforts as a law student in Ottawa, I focused on encouraging Black and racialized youths, mainly from marginalized communities, to consider law as a career option.

The TTC is one of the most iconic institutions within Canada, with a trusted brand known globally. Because of this recognition, combined with my personal story, I was afforded numerous opportunities to speak, mentor, and support programs that focused on youth development. I was cultivating my voice and slowly establishing myself as a leader in the community. The goal was clear, to bring a message of hope and inspiration. My very presence was a demonstration of what was possible for thousands of racialized youths across the GTA. The positive feedback from school officials, parents, students, and community organizations was immediate. I was routinely asked to appear as the keynote speaker at career workshops, graduations, Black History Month events, and youth development training sessions with the likes of CBC anchor Dwight Drummond. With each event, the demand for my services grew. I was grateful to have an employer that understood and supported my initiatives. It was at the TTC that I strengthened my advocacy skills, honed my voice, and discovered my ability to impact others using my platform. My desire to be active in the community was solely motivated by a sense of duty and never by public recognition. Reflecting on my childhood, I knew firsthand how positive reinforcement had changed the trajectory of my life, so I felt obligated to do the same for others.

This type of work always came from the heart. It was never about grabbing the headlines or using this platform to indulge myself personally. Despite doing my best to avoid the limelight, I was honoured to be acknowledged professionally and socially for my work. The year 2011 was monumental for me starting with the TTC Award of Merit in recognition of my outstanding contribution to the TTC, its employees, customers, and the citizens of Toronto. Only a few months later, I was presented with the Government of Canada House of Commons Award for my dedication to community service. The magical year ended on a high note, with a further recognition by the Toronto Star as one of the top fifty Jamaicans in the GTA. The previous two awards were meaningful, but the Toronto Star's acknowledgement was significant because it shed a positive light on my family's birthplace. In many ways, it was the fulfillment of my mother's dreams, having departed from Jamaica to Canada in search of a better life for her children. The recognition was a validation of her values, work ethic, and how she raised her children. My mother would always say, "When you work hard and do things the right way, the recognition will come." As always, she was right.

Early Introduction into Politics

My work in the community continued to centre on supporting youths, families, and educators. However, a tragic community event would formally steer my focus into the world of politics. My first experience working with politicians was after the infamous "Danzig Shooting" in Scarborough in July 2012. The use of weapons was gang related, claiming the lives of several youths at a community barbeque. Shootings were not uncommon in marginalized communities, including Jane and Finch. The continued loss of innocent life left me wanting to do more.

At this point in my life, I was far from the many challenges people face while residing in lower-income communities. I was living comfortably in the upscale suburban community of Oakville. Although far removed, my heart and mind remained with the people in my former community. I desired to be part of the discussion, and potentially the solution, in ending senseless gun violence. I was sitting in my office on a Monday afternoon, when the urge to take immediate action took effect. With a quick Google search, I found MPP Mario Sergio (Yorkview and

York West) and Councillor Anthony Perruzza (Ward 7 Humber River Black Creek). I prepared a well-crafted email with the precision of a litigation lawyer, outlining my background, work performed in the community, and my desire to help. I tapped the send button, unsure of what to expect. After all, I was out of my comfort zone. I was used to working with youths but not with politicians. A few hours later, I was pleasantly surprised to receive a response from both gentlemen.

Both politicians took genuine interest in my comments and invited me to their offices for a face-to-face meeting. Both meetings led to productive discussions, and I left both men excited about the next steps. Following the visits, I was honoured to receive an invitation to join MPP Mario Sergio at a round-table discussion with community leaders and the Youth Services Minister Dr. Eric Hoskins. The meeting would be held at York Gate Mall located in the heart of the Jane and Finch community. Unbeknownst to everyone involved, the event and the location was significant to me. In fact, it was vindication. After receiving the invitation, I had a flashback of attending the mall as a youth with my friends and being followed by security who thought we were there to cause trouble. Fast forward, and I was now returning to the same mall, but this time I was being followed by community leaders and political dignitaries who welcomed my presence and passion to provide hope.

The purpose of the meeting was to hear from community stake-holders and come up with meaningful solutions to curb, and eventually end, the threat of gun violence. There was a call for greater invest-ment in existing community programs and the creation of more job opportunities. When it was my time to speak, I suggested a coordi-nated approach from all levels of government and a commitment to long-term investment, instead of the cut and run tactics marginalized communities were familiar with.

The meeting was engaging and productive. I was proud that I had the opportunity to lend my voice to creating a safe and livable community for our youth. Shortly after the meeting on August 22, 2012, Community Safety Minister Madeleine Meilleur and Children and Youth Services Minister Dr. Eric Hoskins held a press conference, announcing a pledge of $20 million for youth programs in the wake of the deadly shooting. The press release read:

> "Ontario is bolstering crime prevention programs with a focus on youth to the tune of $20 million in an effort to get guns off the streets by trying to prevent kids from turning to crime in the first place."

The intended plan was to expand summer job programs and add more youth outreach workers. My minor role in making such a change opened my eyes to the political process and how it could be used as a vehicle for change. I was comfortable with my community advocacy up to that point, but I felt the overwhelming need to step things up.

Coming into My Own

Working with the TTC, an iconic company I had admired as a child, brought great personal satisfaction. I finally thought I had reached the mountaintop in terms of community impact and success. I was the first person of colour ever hired as a lawyer in the TTC Legal and Claims Department, and who would have blamed me if I had gotten comfortable and called it a career? However, there was more to do and a generation to inspire.

Along the way, I learned that sacrificing my identity was not worth the exchange for perceived acceptance. As a child, I struggled to gain acceptance in my Jamaican family. Eventually finding my place, I vowed never to make the same mistake again. Years later and without giving it much thought, I had broken that promise to myself, resulting in history repeating itself. Once again, I was desperate to be like everyone else instead of my true self. As a racial minority, you can be conditioned to believe that fitting in will help your ascent up the corporate ladder. Without noticing it, you quickly lose your authentic self, becoming a form of contradiction to your race, culture, and beliefs. It was a Caucasian colleague telling me that I was the first Black lawyer hired in the legal department that made me realize that no matter how much I tried to hide my blackness, what I represented was in plain sight for everyone to see. Ultimately, the TTC became more than a job, it was a reminder of the importance of embracing myself wholistically, whether at home or at work. Over the years, I developed a community platform to inspire youths while working with local politicians to bring an end to gun violence in marginalized communities. I had witnessed up close the power and effect of political influence in solving large-scale community issues. I was eager to learn more about politics and politicians. In my pursuit, I never would have imagined that I would be making history all over again.

Chapter 8

A Bold Move Leading to Political History in Shelburne

"The main thing is to make history, not to write it."
– Otto van Bismarck

WITH MY WORK in the community, I had the opportunity to meet people from all walks of life. However, I was excited when I met one of my childhood idols, Canadian Icon Maestro Fresh Wes. While I was impressed by his musical creativity, it was his philosophy on record making that captured my attention. In many of his interviews, he mentioned how young and upcoming artists often approach and ask him how to make the next hit record. The standard response would follow, "Just don't make records, make history." His point was clear: Think big, even if what you are considering has not been done before. In essence, you must be bold, get out of your comfort zone, and strive to leave an unforgettable legacy. The goal is to change lives and not be a flash in a pan. This resonated with me, considering that I had just recently made history at the Toronto Transit Commission and was trying to establish my own legacy.

Figure 8.1: Honoured to be pictured with Maestro Fresh Wes

By the year 2014, I had grown very comfortable in my role as a TTC lawyer and local community advocate. However, I was thirsting for something more. I was ready to make some significant changes in my life. The first step was my decision to leave my comfortable surroundings in Milton, Ontario. I had moved there after selling my first home in Oakville. I was getting good at buying new homes and selling them at the right time for a substantial profit. It was through wise real estate investments that I was able to pay off over $70,000 in student loans in short order.

I was looking for the next profit-making purchase when the Town of Shelburne came on my radar. I was originally planning to purchase a new home in Brampton near my mother, but an afternoon lunchbreak would change everything. I was walking along a quiet residential street when I stopped and picked up a New Home Magazine. On the front cover, it read, "Lakeview Homes in Shelburne, Save $250,000 just north of Brampton." Brampton suddenly went from my preferred destination to my rear-view mirror in just a matter of days. Shelburne was an up-and-coming community and, more importantly, affordable. With my curiosity piqued, I continued to read more intently, learning that Shelburne was only a 35-minute drive north of the City of Brampton on Hwy 10. Feeling a bit adventurous, I took a drive to lay eyes on a community I never knew existed.

The drive up to Shelburne was scenic and calming. It was noticeably different from the hustle and bustle often found on the roads of Milton and Toronto. When I finally arrived in Shelburne, I was first greeted with a sign that welcomed visitors to the Town of Shelburne, population 8500. In comparison to the previous places I had lived, this would be the smallest by a country mile. However, as the saying goes, "Good things come in small packages." As I drove around the town, I fell in love with the abundance of green space, parks, trails, and the friendly people I encountered. I finally made my way to the Sales Centre, where I was welcomed like a family member. After looking at the housing options and floor plans, I left confident that Shelburne would be my new home. Once my mortgage was secured, the decision to move was official.

My move to Shelburne in 2014 coincided with the municipal elections. I thought that God was humouring me, knowing that it was my intention to one day get involved in politics. For a moment, I considered becoming a candidate, after reflecting on my experience working with politicians and the success achieved in the Jane and Finch community. As quickly as the thought entered my mind, it left. The time was not right. I had just moved to this community, and I needed time to get to know the people, their pressing needs, and how I could fit into this equation. Although deciding to sit this one out, I keenly followed the local election in town, as it was a great way to fast-track my knowledge about the community. I read all the campaign pamphlets, attended the townhall debates, and spoke to some of the candidates personally. If I was going to run locally, I now had a good awareness of the issues and a semblance of what was required to run a successful campaign.

The elections came and went, but I yearned for other opportunities to get involved. One evening at home, I saw in the local Shelburne Free Press a call for community members to participate in the Town's Transit Committee. At the time, the Town of Shelburne was exploring all options to extend bus service from Shelburne to Orangeville. During the recent election, I had come to learn that this was a big issue for the community, as many desired public transportation services to connect with educational and employment opportunities outside of town. Shelburne is mainly a commuter's town, and without access to a personal vehicle, getting around is challenging. With my experience working for the largest transportation company in Canada, I was confident in my ability to add value and help resolve this long-standing issue. It was an opportunity I could not refuse. I applied and was happy to receive notice that I had been selected to work with the committee.

At my first meeting, I was brought up to speed by the Town of Shelburne's CAO about previous conversations with GO Transit and the next course of action. The plan was to introduce public transportation through a pilot project, where the town would purchase, operate, and maintain service vehicles. The pilot program was to run for two years. Once success of the program was demonstrated, the goal was to have GO Transit take it over. The whole concept was ambitious but doable because of the increasing demand for public transit. It all made sense, but it was clear from the beginning that GO Transit was reluctant to make any solid commitments. They were concerned that there might not be enough revenue to sustain the route, despite our confidence in the demand for service. They referenced their current arrangement in Orangeville, which had a larger population but still wasn't meeting revenue expectations. Despite Shelburne's growing population at the time, I could see why GO Transit did not share our enthusiasm. Based on my experience, transit discussions can go on for years before service is finally implemented. The fact that we had to be patient to achieve our desired outcome did not take me by surprise. However, it was the question that came next by members of the committee that caught me completely off guard.

It started with a candid discussion about Shelburne growing and being more culturally diverse. Then the question, "What role do you believe town council can play in bringing the newer and more established members of our community together?" That was followed with, "We need to find a way to alleviate any possible tension with the growth of our community." Off the bat, I could tell there was a genuine interest in achieving harmony. This was my first meeting with the group, so I could be forgiven for being stunned. I was not expecting such a question on the Transit Committee. I paused, desperate to come up with something intelligent. Many thoughts raced through my mind: Was this a trick question? Was there something happening in the town that I was not aware of? I was not sure what to say, as I was still relatively new to the Shelburne community. However, not wanting to miss an opportunity to contribute, I spoke about conducting a survey to gauge the thoughts of the community. I also mentioned working with businesses, community organizations, and faith leaders to organize events designed to bring the entire community together. The feedback appeared well-received, and we left the meeting without any follow-up discussion on the topic. At the time, I never would have guessed that this would define my legacy in Shelburne for years to come.

With each passing day, I continued to learn more about, and grow more comfortable with, the community I called home. In addition to my bold decision to move from my comfort zone in Milton, Ontario, I was also seeking opportunities for professional development. In 2014, I was honoured to be appointed for a three-year term by the provincial government as a Public Member for the Ontario College of Kinesiologists. I applied for this position knowing that my son, Devante, was a student in the Kinesiology Program at the University of Toronto. I was hopeful that my appointment, and the knowledge obtained along the way, would provide him with some value. In this role, I worked with other public appointees and members of the profession elected to serve.

This was my first introduction into the world of corporate governance at this level, but I embraced the opportunity to learn something new. The committee structure, responsibilities, and financial realities closely resembled that of a municipal council. Elected leaders were expected to represent and respond to the growing needs of their community but were often constrained by limited budgets. Similarly, we were picked to help respond to the needs of the College, professional members, and the public. As a committee, our actions were mainly guided by the state of the College's finances. Government funding was limited and often temporary, so we learned very quickly the meaning of fiscal prudence. The balancing act of managing funds, securing new revenue sources, while attempting to meet the expectations of those we served, kept us all on our toes for the entire three-year term.

At the end of my tenure, I was re-appointed in 2017. At the beginning of each term, it is customary to elect the President, Vice-President, and Chairs of various subcommittees for the College. The process was highly political. If you were interested in running for a position, you had to fill out a nomination form along with signatures of support. At the appropriate time, each candidate would be given the opportunity to deliver a two-to-three-minute speech before the committee, articulating why they were the best person for the role. The process and the game plan were simple: To be successful, you had to secure enough votes to obtain your desired position.

The last time I had participated in an election format like this was in my first year at the University of Detroit Mercy Law School. It was there that I ran for, and was elected, class vice-president. My current pursuit would be equally challenging and nerve-racking. Thankfully, I had the memory of prior success to motivate me. Along with some encouragement from other committee members, I set my sights on becoming the next Vice-President and Chair of the Discipline Committee. Pursuing the role of vice-president was certainly a bold move, considering it was customary for senior committee members to pursue this position. However, I was there to challenge myself and to demonstrate my leadership capabilities. With little time to waste, I immediately rolled up my sleeves and got to work. I spent the following days speaking to my fellow committee members, sharing my vision, answering questions, and doing my best to rally support. Before I knew it, the brief campaign period had ended. At our next scheduled meeting, the winners would be formally declared. In the interim, this was the only thing that occupied my mind. I consistently questioned whether I had done enough to achieve my desired outcome. Ultimately, I settled on the feeling that the experience, win or lose, would provide growth.

The day arrived and the election was the first thing on the committee agenda. There was a stillness in the room before each candidate was given an opportunity to make a final pitch. I went last and passionately laid out my vision for the respective roles I had chosen. Once I concluded my remarks, it was time to vote. Each committee member placed their selection into a box before it was whisked away into another room to be counted by the College staff. The wait was agonizing. There was nervous chatter as everyone waited for the results. I kept quiet, deciding to pass the time reading an inspirational quote on my phone. Despite my best efforts to block out the noise, I could still overhear committee members making predictions on the outcome of each position. My sense of calm dissipated and my anxiety rose sharply with each passing prediction.

Finally, the staff members returned to salvage my mental sanity. They proceeded to thank everyone for their participation and went straight to the results. The College Registrar went through each position, announcing each successful candidate. Once the victor was identified, each committee member nodded and clapped in approval. This continued until it came to the positions that I had campaigned for. I sensed that the position for Vice-President was going to be called next, so I put my head down and whispered a prayer. Before I could finish, I heard, "For the position of Vice-President, Steve Anderson." I abruptly snapped my head back up to a round of applause.

After thanking the committee, I sat silently, trying to process what had just happened. I barely managed to do that before I heard my name being called again for the Chair of the Discipline Committee. This time, I was able to generate a smile for everyone to see. I was honoured that my fellow peers trusted me to lead in these high-profile positions. When it was all over, I took the time to thank the other candidates, congratulating them on a good campaign. One of the staff members leaned over and said, "Do you know that you are the first Black Vice-President and Chair of the Discipline Committee?" At this point in my story, I know what you are thinking. "This sounds very familiar." You are right! When I was told, I had the feeling of déjà vu. It was just a few short years prior that one of my colleagues at the TTC had shared a similar fact about my ground-breaking hire in the legal department.

Words could not describe the sense of accomplishment I felt. However, at the same time, I began to wonder how this was possible. How could I be the first? I was certain that there were many other people who looked like me who were just as qualified. The moment suddenly felt bittersweet, because it was a recognition that many were likely not getting a fair opportunity. I began to question my own success, wondering, "Why me?" and, "What did I do to deserve this and not someone else?" I had always believed in my own work ethic and capabilities, but it became clear to me that having a good education and strong work ethic was not enough for some to secure meaningful opportunities. I understood how systemic barriers and prejudice held people back in marginalized communities like Jane and Finch, but I was surprised to sense that this may be happening in the corporate world as well. I was honoured to be recognized in this special way, but the joy of hearing that I was the first had now faded away. I was more determined than ever to make sure the door would be open for many others who were just as qualified. To do that, I was convinced that I had to do something different. After my hire as a full-time lawyer with the TTC, I focused on using my platform to help and inspire students to consider law as a career. Following this recent experience, it reminded me of my desire to expand my platform to help more people. I would soon get the opportunity to stand on the biggest stage of my life.

2018 Municipal Elections

Brimming with confidence from my election win at the Ontario College of Kinesiologists, I set my sights on the 2018 Municipal Elections. My decision to enter politics was never about hoarding power or prestige; I was satisfied with my professional and community accomplishments up to that point. This run, in large part, was about inspiring and creating opportunities for a segment of society often overlooked. After serving the community of Shelburne in several volunteer roles, I had the privilege to learn about the people and the issues they faced. Municipal politics appealed to me, as I would not be handcuffed by the party agendas and demand for loyalty often found at the provincial and federal level. I would have more flexibility to follow through on the issues that really mattered to me. Thinking optimistically, I visualized using my political platform to ensure equity, equality, and fair treatment for all peoples.

My experience growing up in the Jane and Finch community and the instances of bias and stereotyping experienced early in my legal career were the driving forces behind this mindset. If there were systemic barriers preventing members from marginalized communities from accessing services and employment opportunities, I wanted to change that. I had plenty of ideas running through my head, but I had no experience in how to plan and run a successful political campaign. Fortunately, I had some time to get organized, or so I thought.

It was a Thursday evening at home when I picked up a copy of the Shelburne Free Press from the coffee table. I was only a couple of pages into my read, when I came across some shocking news that would change my timeline for action. The article referred to the tragic passing of one of Shelburne's beloved and longstanding councillors, Tom Egan. This caught me and the entire community by surprise. After adjusting to the initial shock, I continued to read the rest of the article. Towards the end, it mentioned that his councillor's seat would be vacated and that the Town of Shelburne was seeking a replacement through a formal nomination process. One can only imagine my state of emotions; I was sad and yet cautiously optimistic for the opportunity that was ahead. Councillor Egan was experienced and well-respected. Anyone seeking to replace him would first have to convince all of town council before attempting to fill his mighty big shoes.

After putting down the paper, the first set of voices in my head told me that the town would want to replace Tom Egan with someone who was also very well-known, someone that could easily fit in. At the time, Shelburne Council did not represent the growing diversity in the town. According to the Statistics Canada 2016, Shelburne was the fastest growing town in Ontario and the second fastest in Canada per population ratio. Shelburne was also identified as the most ethnically diverse community in the County of Dufferin.

However, a simple Google search revealed that Council was made up entirely of older white men with deep roots in the community. I later learned, after speaking to one of my neighbours, that the Town of Shelburne had never had a person of colour serve on its Council since it was founded by William Jelly in the 1860s. One could effectively argue that it was the unbreakable good old boys' club. As a result, none of the images of Tom Egan's replacement that entered my mind resembled what I saw in the mirror. It was clear that the odds were significantly against me. I had the monumental task of shifting Council's attention away from the obvious fact that I was different. The goal was to have them focus on my credentials and ideas, making it easier to view me as a suitable replacement for Councillor Egan. Thinking about the magnitude of the opportunity, I was certain that my appointment to Council would be a bold statement to onlookers that young Black men can achieve success beyond the stereotypical box of sports and entertainment.

As a youngster, I never saw a Black politician in the Jane and Finch community or on television. As a result, I spent much of my youth thinking that politics was not a realistic career option. The decision to enter politics went beyond perception of power and prestige. At the core, it was about showcasing the diverse talent in the Black community and what is possible if given an opportunity.

If successful, my presence in this position of authority would inspire and empower the growing Black and racialized community in Shelburne and the County of Dufferin. Unlike the surprises of my historic achievements with the Toronto Transit Commission and the Ontario College of Kinesiologists, I was fully aware of what was at stake and the history to be made with my appointment. No matter how daunting, I could not refuse the opportunity to establish a legacy and prove that no career option is off limits because of where you live, your skin colour, gender, or religion. The date was set by the Shelburne Town Council: a special meeting was to be held in Council Chambers on October 2, 2017 at 7:00 PM to name Councillor Egan's replacement. I started to prepare without telling anyone, because I did not need the additional pressure.

October 2nd arrived faster than I had anticipated. The day started out like any other day, until the clock approached 6:00 PM. I went from feeling calm to suddenly feeling nervous. I did my best to downplay the moment in my mind but could not shake what was at stake. I decided it was best to pray and ask God to be a source of strength. Feeling better, I put on my power suit and proceeded to town hall. As I entered Council Chambers, it was filled with members of the community and the local press who were present to learn of Councillor Egan's replacement. Among the attendees was his surviving wife and children. Like a wide-eyed child in a candy store, I surveyed the room and quickly noticed that I was the only visible minority among the other Caucasian candidates. I was not shocked by this observation; I had grown accustomed to being the only Black or racialized person present the further I advanced in my education and professional endeavours. However, I almost turned around and left the building when I witnessed one of the candidates having a friendly conversation with a Councillor before the session started.

I began to feel I was wasting my time. Did the Council already know who they wanted? Was the decision already made? The person I saw speaking to the Councillor appeared to fit the profile I had imagined the Council and the community wanted to replace Councillor Egan with. Needing to refocus, I stepped out of the room and found a quiet place in the hallway. With time to think, I recalled my time on the town's Transit Committee and the question I was asked about how to bring the Shelburne community together. It really did not resonate back then, but my very presence that evening and potential appointment to Council would go a long way in accomplishing that desired outcome.

The town clerk came into the hallway and gathered the attention of all the candidates. We were informed that we would be called into Council Chambers one by one, with fifteen minutes to present and answer questions. After addressing us, she disappeared back into the room. Then began the nervous chatter amongst the group as we waited for our names to be called. As I waited for my turn, I took my wallet out of my pocket and stared at the picture of my children. I would usually do this in big moments to remind myself why the effort and the sacrifice were necessary. It worked every time. After the third candidate had entered and left the Council Chambers, the town clerk appeared and said, "Mr. Anderson, please come into Council Chambers and join us." There was no turning back. This was my moment to shine.

I entered the room and immediately noticed that everyone was looking in my direction. After all, it was hard for me to go undetected. I stood six-feet-three-inches with a dark complexion, sporting one of my custom-made suits with a bright red pocket square for good measure. I felt the intense looks of curiosity and amazement as each set of eyes tracked my every movement. It was as if a black unicorn had just entered the room. The feeling reminded me of my first few court appearances and hearings with the TTC. The stares by some over the years clearly revealed their inward feeling of surprise that I had achieved such a level of success. To be fair, in this present situation, I was still new and relatively unknown in the community, so that likely explained part of the reaction.

I had fifteen minutes to make my best pitch. To make matters more strenuous, members of the Egan family were seated in the reserved seats for members of the public and media directly behind me. With the clock ticking, the questions came fast and furious. Never one to dodge, I answered each question with a thoughtful and measured response.

In my mind, I could not get over the feeling of being involved in a speed dating session. I was seducing Council to pick me over the next candidate for the position. If I was going to make a lasting impression, I had to make my time memorable.

The areas of discussion were broad, ranging from my understanding of the community, my ideas on how to bring the diverse community together, and what I saw as the future of Shelburne. I answered each question directly, making eye contact with each member of Council. I was always told as a child to make eye contact with the person I was speaking with. Direct eye contact is often used to assess credibility and character. As the session went on, my comfort level began to increase. With each answer, I observed a lot of head-nodding and note-taking. The session ended with the question, "What is the first thing you would do if you were appointed to Council?" Without hesitation, I stated that within my first ten days in office, I would establish the Tom Egan Community Service Award to be given annually to deserving members of the community. The response drew a few smiles and a thumbs up from one of the Councillors.

With my final response given, my fifteen-minute session was over. During my interview, the entire Chamber was silent, only pierced with Council's questions and my responses. When I got out of my chair and turned to leave the room, something happened that I never expected. The entire public gallery behind me erupted in applause. I was completely shocked but kept my composure. I faced the gallery with a smile and said, "Thank you," before exiting the room. Following the warm response, I briefly allowed myself to imagine being seated around the Council table, making decisions on the behalf of the community. Following my session, two more candidates were interviewed before we were all called back into the room to witness the voting and hear the final decision. The public gallery grew more crowded as additional chairs were brought in to accommodate the candidates.

I nervously entered the room and took a seat next to some of my competitors. With the chairs closely positioned next to each other, I could hear and feel the breathing of the people around me. There was an eerie silence as everyone waited to hear the outcome. The tension was building when the town clerk finally announced, "I will tally the votes and, in a moment, I will reveal who has been appointed to Council."

With those words, she had my attention, along with everyone else's in the room. For small town politics, it was certain that this decision would reverberate throughout the entire community for the weeks and months ahead. If I were appointed, the political establishment would never be the same again, and I would make sure of that. At the time, I was unclear whether Council had truly considered what it would mean to appoint me, as I was never one for rubber stamping or concealing my opinions. I was relatively young, full of energy, and determined to take decisive action for the betterment of our community. Were they ready for a person like me? I was going to find out. With that, the town clerk said, "The votes have been counted and Steve Anderson has been appointed to Council."

What? Who? Where? Me? My eyes almost popped out of my head!

Applause engulfed the room as each Council member stood up and took turns congratulating me. I must have passed out at some point, because I do not remember much after shaking many hands and saying thank you a million times. However, there was a moment that I won't soon forget. Among the throngs of people, members of the Egan family came over to congratulate me with a warm embrace. The encounter was emotional for all of us. I remember looking them in their eyes, promising that I would do my best to honour Councillor Egan's memory, while making them and the rest of the community proud. I left the town hall that evening determined to keep my promise. When I arrived home, I opened the front door and immediately went down on my knees, thanking God for giving me the fortitude, wisdom, and strength to get through this moment.

Once I was finished, I got up and ran to the phone to call my children, Asia and Devante, to share the news. Most of the call was filled with screams, laughter, and their repeating how proud they were of me. I called my mother, who prayed and thanked God for giving me this special opportunity. Through the tears and joy, we reflected on my journey and concluded that I had been directed to Shelburne for this very moment. Considering that I had never heard of Shelburne prior to moving there, it was obvious that she was right. None of this was supposed to be possible for a skinny kid from Jane and Finch, but here we were again, celebrating how I was able to overcome the odds.

I barely slept that night as a stream of thoughts raced through my mind. I reflected on the political giants I had come to learn about, such as the Honourable Jean Augustine and the Honourable Lieutenant Governor of Ontario Lincoln Alexander—both trailblazers breaking down barriers and paving the way for others. Their achievements serve as an immense source of pride for many in the Black community. In my own small way, I was doing the same for the Black community in Shelburne and the County of Dufferin.

The journey to that point was certainly not easy. However, the bumps in the road, the setbacks, the disappointments, and the achievements all prepared me for this moment in my life. I was now on the biggest stage of my life, with political influence and the responsibility to be an example that the community could be proud of. As daunting as this realization was in my mind, I was ready for it. The next day, I received a call from staff at town hall advising me that my swearing-in ceremony was scheduled for October 16, 2017, just outside Council Chambers. Before I could process the phone call and the details of the date, I received another call from a friend who asked if I had read what the mayor had said in the Shelburne Free Press. I was suddenly nervous and unsure of the nature of the comment. Was I already in trouble before I officially started?

My friend sent me a screenshot of the quote, " 'He just seemed to be the most prepared, the most confident,' the mayor said. 'He had some great new ideas for inclusion in our new diverse community. He was just a step ahead of the rest.' " I was honoured by the words but had no time to relish the moment, as the swearing-in ceremony was just around the corner. I was excited to find out that my brother Clive would be flying in from Singapore to join the rest of my family at the event. I was also thankful that my childhood friends, Ian Daley and Andrew Guy, would be present to participate in the celebration. These guys had supported me every step of the way, so it was important that they were there to share in the moment.

October 16, 2017 was one of the best moments in my life, as I was sworn in before a packed room of supporters. Life, from that moment on, would never be the same.

The next few days, and the weeks to follow, were a whirlwind of media interviews, speaking requests, and invitations to community gatherings, big and small. I was exhausted, but I knew what I was getting into the moment I sought the appointment to Council. I would use each encounter to share my vision, while listening to the needs and concerns of those in our community. I was excited for the work ahead and the opportunity to improve the lives of everyone in our small town. Some suggested that I was politically naive in my desire to help every single person, but I was sincerely committed to doing what was best for our community. After all, if I did not plan on being there for the people, I should just step aside and make room for someone who would.

Each person I met was quick to remind me of the significance of my appointment. It was viewed as a sign of progress and acceptance for a small conservative town. Although true, historical achievements are not without their hurdles, as making history is only a part of the

Figure 8.2: At my swearing in ceremony surrounded by family

journey. Being the first racialized person to hold this office came with a lot of recognition and praise, but it also came with an immense amount of pressure unlikely felt by my fellow elected colleagues.

The moment I raised my right hand at my swearing-in ceremony and accepted the terms of the office, the weight of the position hit me hard. I had experienced a similar feeling when I became the first Black lawyer ever hired in the TTC Legal Department. Now in public office, the stakes were even higher, with an entire community depending on my every move. Knowing that every decision could materially impact someone's life added to the internal pressure to perform. I felt the added stress to be superhuman, to avoid disappointing the community and, in particular, members from my own race. I was always mindful not to do anything that would ruin the future opportunity for another Black person looking to travel the same road. Even though my political responsibilities would be far different than my role at the TTC, I was, in many respects, reliving what it felt like to navigate in predominately Caucasian spaces. In these instances, it is often difficult to be your authentic self, resulting in a feeling of loneliness and isolation. I was committed to being myself, but it was hard to ignore the fact that I was once again surrounded by individuals who could not relate to my experiences of being a Black man. The importance of diversity, inclusion, and equity cannot be overstated. If successfully implemented in all sectors across our society, it will immediately release the pressure and stresses that come with being the only one.

With no immediate changes on the horizon, I internalized my feelings, never wanting to seem weak or unable to handle the rollercoaster ride of politics. I was riding high following my appointment to Council, but it was lonely at the top. The time to figure out my internal issues would have to wait. I had a lot to learn and connections to make in ten short months before the next election. The mission was clear, I had to work harder than anyone else on Council to prove that my appointment was not in error.

I was fortunate to hit the ground running, participating in several community initiatives, which included the creation and presentation of the Councillor Tom Egan Community Service Award, honouring our war veterans by laying the Provincial Wreath, a privilege bestowed upon me by MPP Sylvia Jones, celebrating milestone birthdays of our seniors in long-term care facilities, and partnering with Bell Canada to provide brand new backpacks to underprivileged children in our community. Additionally, within my first few months on Council, I successfully brought a motion forward to have the town formally acknowledge and celebrate major cultural events such as Black History Month, Ramadan, Eid, Diwali, and many others through print ads, social media, and the mayor's newsletter. With each passing day, I was getting more confident and comfortable in my new role. Early signs suggested that

Figure 8.3: Council Tom Egan Community Service Award Recipient
Dorian Jeffrey-Jones and members of the Egan family

the community was getting more comfortable and confident in my
abilities as well.

I was finally getting a handle on how to deal with my historic achievement and the pressures that came with it. Little did I know that lightning
would strike twice, forcing me to start the learning curve all over again.

Chapter 9

Lightning Strikes Twice

"Be the lightning even if it is for a second time."
– Unknown

WITH THE 2018 municipal elections around the corner, I was hoping to rely on old and new alliances in my bid to secure public office, again. During my brief ten months on Council, I got a front row seat on how working with, and on behalf of, the community can produce favourable results. I was hungry for the opportunity to do a lot more. Along with the good, the pending elections would reveal the ugly side of politics, which took me by surprise. Despite having strong support of Council and the community, I was hearing whispers in some corners that perhaps my appointment in 2017 was a fluke, as I did not run a full election campaign and the community did not elect me. Social media posts suggested that I was the Milli Vanilli of politics. A one-trick pony who did not stand a chance against stiff competition in the upcoming elections. The fact that I was not born and raised in Shelburne was an issue of concern. I was considered part of the infiltration from Brampton. Change can be difficult in any community. It was my responsibility to show that my presence was not a threat, but represented change for the better. With all my accomplishments, I was not immune to criticism. As a public official, I was open to legitimate critiques based on my record, but some of the comments I saw on social media had darker undertones.

Over the years, I had come to learn that my achievements in life would never afford me a period of rest. As a Black man, I constantly had to break free from the stereotypes and biases that stalked me like an uninvited shadow. It was Frederick Douglass, an American social reformer and statesman, who said:

> "Though the coloured man is no longer subject to be bought and sold, he is still surrounded by an adverse sentiment which fetters all his movements. In his downward course he meets with no resistance, but his course upward is resented and resisted at every step of his progress. If he comes in ignorance, rags, and wretchedness, he conforms to the popular belief of his character, and in that character he is welcome. But if he shall come as a gentleman, a scholar, and a statesman, he is hailed a contradiction to his race. The colour line meets him everywhere, and in a measure shuts him out from all respectable and profitable trades and callings."

Being born Black meant spending the rest of my life defending my worth and staying power. In essence, I was destined to live my life as Black Superman. Showing incredible strength, the ability to achieve beyond expectations, and a willingness to accept my role without question are qualities I would consistently have to display, just to be seen as worthy for everyday opportunities. Anything less would certainly relegate me to a life of mediocrity or worse. The freedom to navigate life like Clark Kent would never be an option. The plan was to use the upcoming elections to prove once more what I was capable of. I longed for the day when my skin colour would not be a controlling factor in how others perceived me. However, being realistic, I knew such a thought was only wishful thinking for now.

As my short political stint was winding to a close, I noticed a change in dynamics around the Council table. As a newcomer to this political arena, I was surprised that no one was willing to reveal their future intentions to run again, at least not right away. It is hard to explain, but I caught on to a tension not observed during my tenure on Council up to that point. The calculated silence around the Council table did not stop the community from speculating on who should run again or be voted out. The online chatter and the coffee shops were heating up with discussions about local issues, the direction of the town and, of course, the performance of each member on Council. Over the course of your term, you could expect to get trickles of feedback, good or bad, on how you were performing. Truthfully, you were never sure whether the commentary was representative of the entire community. Unlike in the educational system, there is no formal midterm report card grading your performance in municipal politics. A true evaluation of any political figure comes every four years, when the community chooses who they want to see in office for the next four years. I was proud of the work I had accomplished in the ten months since my appointment, and I was hopeful about my chances of being elected as a Councillor. What appeared to be the path of least resistance was turned upside-down with the upcoming unexpected turn of events.

Only a few weeks had passed following the date that members of Council and the community could formally register their intention to run for public office, when the atomic bomb was dropped. The Mayor and Deputy Mayor shockingly decided not to seek re-election. Both men had served on Council for many years, and just like that, they signalled their exit. The political landscape, to borrow a line from music icon Elvis Presley, "Was all shook up." New leadership was up for grabs. For a small town like Shelburne, this was juicy front-page news. The political intensity, drama, and community banter reached feverish heights, and it was now game on.

You could cut the tension around the Council table with a knife as we attempted to grapple with the pending departure of the Mayor and Deputy Mayor, all the while mulling over our own political futures. Each move here on out would have to be calculated and carefully thought out. If one moved too quickly to replace these men, it could have been seen as a power grab and offensive to a segment of the community. For the first few weeks after the bombshell announcement, nobody did a thing, at least not publicly. I was a political rookie, and any misstep would have surely derailed my future political ambitions in this town. Should I seek re-election as a Councillor or do the unthinkable and run for Mayor or Deputy Mayor?

I relied heavily on my Spiderman-like senses to observe my surroundings and guide my steps. Quite frankly, I had no choice, because the remaining members of Council kept their own future ambitions close to their chests. As we all contemplated our next moves privately, we got more shocking news when one of the longest serving Councillors announced he would not seek re-election. It felt like the ground was consistently shifting under my feet. This was the first time I was experiencing such a dramatic election turn over. I never could have planned for such a wild ride. I know the community must have felt the same, because over the past twenty years, there were only minor changes to the makeup of Council. The elections in Shelburne were often as predictable as butter melting on hot toast. The community was largely conditioned to the same names and faces running the town politically. The biggest shake-up came with my appointment to Council in 2017, but the main core remained intact.

I had given considerable thought to my next move, speaking to family, friends, and people with political experience that could help direct me. The success following my appointment to Council could not mask the image I saw every time I stood in front of the mirror. Based on the whispers I was hearing, what I looked like and represented posed a problem for some. To have any chance in a campaign bid for Mayor or Deputy Mayor, I would have to devise the perfect game plan. Any less of an effort for such a bold move would have me laughed right out of town.

Running for the head of Council, considering that I had only served on Council for ten months, would certainly grab the headlines. This was going to be the biggest splash the town had ever seen. I was quietly told by some people that Shelburne might not be ready for a Black Mayor or Deputy Mayor. It was only a short time ago that the community had to grapple with having their first Black Councillor in the town's history. Despite the feedback, I remained confident, knowing the welcoming and progressive nature of the community. Whatever the choice, I was banking on each person seeing and judging me on my substance and nothing else.

As I continued to ponder my next move, I received a surprise phone call from a fellow Councillor wanting to talk about the elephant in the room—the upcoming municipal elections. He was young, smart, ambitious, and had a sincere regard for the community and its direction. We had mutual respect and clicked instantly on our shared vision for the community. Before we hung up the phone, it was clear what I needed to do. I made the courageous decision to run and seek the community's support to become the next Deputy Mayor. I knew my decision would cause a stir within the community, but the timing felt right. This decision was not about power but principle. I wanted to ensure that Shelburne remained a welcoming community while catapulting its status as leader in the County of Dufferin and beyond.

There are moments in our lives when we stall progress because we are fearful of the unknown or the likelihood of defeat. If we succumb

Figure 9.1: With Councillor Wade Mills after both filing our election papers

to those feelings, it is assured that we will miss out on opportunities to grow, learn, and impact the lives of others in a positive way. If I wanted my vision for the community to come to fruition, I needed to step up and out of my comfort zone. I was unwilling to let fear of the unknown dissuade me from what had to be done. The choice by the current Mayor and Deputy Mayor not to seek re-election signalled an opportunity for the community to move in a new direction. It was now up to me to seize the opportunity to lead.

On July 28, 2018, I filed my papers at town hall, publicly declaring my intention to become Shelburne's next Deputy Mayor. That felt like the easy part. I now had to prepare for the onslaught I knew was coming my way.

It did not take very long for the news about my decision to spread through the community. I was accepted by most when I was appointed as a Councillor, but the audacity to seek the second most powerful position in the town would only serve to intensify the level of scrutiny and criticism I was already hearing. At that point, I had lived in Shelburne for approximately four years, but the talk of being an outsider was getting louder and louder. I was left to interpret that I was not fit nor qualified to hold the office of Deputy Mayor. While it was true that I was still new compared to the more established residents, I would not allow anyone to question my commitment to the town. I was cognizant that people were just getting used to me as their first Black Councillor, and for some, my climb to the top of the hill was happening too fast.

To be Shelburne's next Deputy Mayor, I would have to overcome a tremendous amount to have an opportunity to lead. I was determined to do just that by placing my values, integrity, and vision for the community at the front and centre of my campaign. Under my leadership, Shelburne would be a community where no one would feel excluded or left behind. Our success would depend on everyone pulling in the same direction and equally sharing in the rewards. During my term on Council, I was fortunate to have credibility and the trust of the community after leading several successful initiatives. I was counting on these same people to see me do the same and more in the role of Deputy Mayor.

Understanding the work that laid ahead, I assembled an all-star team of volunteers who, alongside me, took my message to the community one door at a time. In addition to my team, I made the calculated move to also knock on doors with a fellow senior Councillor who was well-known and highly respected in the community. We both shared a bold and inclusive vision for the town, so it made our pairing easy. I valued the time spent with him, asking a lot of questions and soaking up every bit of information he was willing to give. I learned a lot about the community, the history of the town, and how to run a successful

Figure 9.2: Out placing my elections signs

campaign. I was the happy and eager student wanting to learn from one of the best in the business. After all, he had been elected and served on Council for over twenty years, so I certainly felt I was in good hands.

The campaign period ran from July up until the vote on October 22, 2018. As it was my first stab at a community-wide election campaign, I was unprepared for how gruelling, mentally and physically, the whole experience would be. The weather conditions ranged from extremely hot to extremely cool as we approached October. Even with the elements, I was out most days, taking my message to every household in Shelburne. If I wanted to be victorious, I had no choice. I was up against stiff competition, as a fellow incumbent Councillor and popular community organizer was also seeking the position of Deputy Mayor. This was going to be a battle of the ages. The scene was set for the audience: It was the newcomer against the well-known and established brand. It was the biblical David versus Goliath story, and, like David, there were many who did not believe I stood a chance against the mighty giant.

My fellow Councillor and I had two very distinct visions for the town, and it was my job to have the community walk the path I was proposing. Along the way, some well-intended supporters pleaded that I reconsider my run for Deputy Mayor and opt to run for Councillor instead. This was seen as an easier path, considering the odds I was up against. Even though it appeared they were looking out for my best interest, I immediately rejected the suggestion. At this point, there was no turning back. I was fully prepared to live with the outcome of my decision.

Although brave in heart and mind, when it came to facing my opponent, I dreaded the door-knocking portion of the campaign, because it was hard to gauge what would happen once the door opened. Even though I spent many days knocking on doors with a fellow Caucasian Councillor, it did not shield me from some of the things to come. On the outside, I was always mindful to show unbreakable confidence. However, on the inside, I quietly questioned whether I would be accepted or rejected for reasons other than my message. Despite my typically optimistic attitude, it was difficult not to think about this as I approached each door. The reality was, I did not have the luxury to simply ignore what I looked like and how others would perceive me. Unfortunately, what I dreaded the most became my reality. I did experience clear displays of racism while canvassing in the community, which made me question whether it was worth it to continue. Nobody wants to feel put down for trying to do something positive. While the encounters were discouraging, I took comfort in knowing that most people were good-hearted and welcoming. By no means is my story unique to Shelburne. Racialized persons looking to get involved in politics must often consider, weigh, ponder, and make decisions based on factors unrelated to the substance of their message. In the face of challenges, I was never one to use perceived barriers as an excuse not to succeed. In short order, I gathered myself and I took my message of hope, trust, and prosperity to every door, whether I was welcomed or not.

With each door-knocking session, public meet-and-greet, and debate, my confidence began to grow. The feedback from residents of all backgrounds was encouraging. Many provided reassurance that I belonged and confirmed that I had secured their vote. For the first time during the campaign, I took a moment to consider the possibilities of what an election victory would mean for me and the community. I was happy with the positive feedback; however, there was no time to take my foot off the gas. By all accounts, the battle for the position of Deputy Mayor was going right down to the wire. We were fighters, having invested our time, energy, and resources.

On Council, we were cordial and respectful to one another, but we were certainly not friends. We had a mutual respect, but it was clear from the beginning of the election campaign that neither of us was prepared to concede an inch. With numerous positions up for grabs around the Council table, this was the position that captured the attention of the community and media the most. This was my biggest professional challenge to date, and I treated it as such. To be honest, I wanted this badly to prove to myself and the critics that I could run a full campaign and be successful. It was not easy knowing that results could go either way. With only days to go, there was still no clear winner in the court of public opinion. With all the talk about how close the result was going to be, no one could have predicted the photo finish right around the corner.

With the last election flyer handed out, I took a moment to reflect on the four months of the campaign; it was certainly a rollercoaster ride of highs and lows. Regardless of the outcome, I was proud of the campaign I had run and equally proud of the people who supported me every step of the way. That said, the whole ordeal took a mental and physical toll on me. Unless you have done this yourself, it is hard to appreciate the sacrifices that need to be made to run a successful campaign. For many days, weeks, and months, I sacrificed time with family and friends and put a hold on other personal interests. Ultimately, one accepts this as part of the territory when you sign up, but it was still difficult to deal with.

Judgment Day

October 22, 2018 was election day. I spent a portion of the day knocking on doors and making phone calls to make sure that my supporters were able to get out and vote. Although members of our community had the ease of voting electronically for the first time, the work to get people to follow up with their stated commitment was still intense. I spent the remainder of the day quietly at home, knowing that my life could potentially change in a matter of hours. I consciously made the decision to be alone that evening to avoid raising my anxiety level and that of those around me while waiting for the votes to be counted and the winners announced. It was difficult to eat, take a nap, or focus on anything else, because I knew the decision was fast approaching. In the moment, I felt helpless knowing there was nothing more I could do to influence the decision. I had put in the work over the last four months, and I had to trust that it was enough.

Each candidate was given the opportunity to attend town hall and watch the live vote come in, but I did not have the nerves to handle being in that environment. Regardless of the result, I wanted to have the time to process everything alone before encountering other people and the list of questions that would predictably follow. My heartbeat and stress level went off the charts when the polls were formally closed. The only thing left was to count the votes and declare the winner.

All the candidates were previously told that they would receive a call from a member of town staff once the winners were declared. Listening for that phone call, you could hear particles of dust fall to the floor. That was how quiet it was in my house. As the clock ticked away, I received many false alarms from well wishers and those simply looking for a status update. This went on for about an hour following the closing of the polls. I was an emotional wreck each time the phone rang. With the next call, I was ready to snap, letting out my frustrations on the poor soul. I knew I would later regret my actions, but in the moment, I was not my usual calm self. Sure enough, the phone rang again, and I answered, clearly agitated. "I don't know the decision yet. I will let you know when I find out." I blurted that out without first finding out the identity of the caller. When I finally paused to give the person an opportunity to speak, it was a voice I immediately recognized as one of my Councillor colleagues. The next thing I remember hearing was, "You did it. You are the next Deputy Mayor for the Town of Shelburne."

I do not remember if I said a word in response. With my knees trembling, I took a seat on the couch. I barely had time to process what had just happened, as my phone rang repeatedly with those eager to congratulate me on this historic achievement. I had just become the first Black Deputy Mayor after just becoming the town's first Black Councillor only ten months earlier. I ultimately learned that the race for Deputy Mayor was closer than anyone had ever imagined. I had won by 27 votes. Yes, 27 votes!

When watching previous elections on television, I would hear experienced politicians say that every vote counts. This fact could not have been truer in my situation. Never taking a vote for granted, my team and I knocked on every door in town. The hard work, determination, and commitment paid off. Due to an unexpected twist, my celebration that evening would be placed on pause. Because of the close margin of victory, I was told that the result would be subject to an automatic recount that evening. My emotions would have a seat on another roller-coaster. Many thoughts crossed my mind as I waited for confirmation. Had there been a mistake? Would I end up losing the vote? What would I say to all my supporters? Fortunately, I would not have to find out the answers to those questions. Within an hour, I received a call informing me that the vote recount yielded the same result.

Once the dust had settled, I took the opportunity to call my campaign team, family, and friends to thank them all. These core folks had stuck with me from the very beginning and were unwavering in their support. The four-month campaign had many highs and lows that tested my will, mentally and physically. I was grateful for all the support, because I certainly needed it.

With the hard part behind me, I was now fully in party mode. That evening, a lot of people descended on my house to celebrate. There was a steady flow of mineral water poured into large and small shot glasses (my mom and children will be reading this book) followed by reminiscing, laughter, and tears, acknowledging what this achievement meant for the community. I got out of my comfort zone and did something I never imagined was possible growing up in Jane and Finch—and that was running an election campaign and winning. As a youth, discussions around politics were reserved for people who did not look like me. In my wildest dreams, I never would have imagined that this achievement was possible. With my election victory, I was determined to use my platform to ensure that no other Black or racialized youth would feel the same way.

I reflected on what could only be described as unbelievable, yet a dream come true. The underdog beating the odds to achieve success is a story normally reserved for Hollywood blockbuster movies. Fortunately, this was no movie; it was my life in the small Town of Shelburne. With little political experience, labelled a fluke by some following my appointment to Council in 2017, I was now widely seen as a model of success to be admired and emulated.

Figure 9.3: Officially becoming the Deputy Mayor

Just like my successful appointment to Council, I once again carefully reflected on the Black trailblazers before me, all of whom had broken down racial and systemic barriers to make this achievement possible. I knew the best way I could honour their sacrifices was to continue to pave the way, creating opportunities for others.

The celebration at my home continued well into the evening, with good conversation, music, and plenty of photos to capture the moment. For the first time in a long while, I allowed myself to freely bask in the moment, knowing that the expectations and the work ahead would consume my time and thoughts for the next four years. The evening ended with hugs, kisses, and hearing how I had made each person proud. I took every comment seriously. As a child, you often want to validate the efforts and sacrifices of your parents with your achievements. Considering everything my family had done for me, this was my way of showing that their efforts were not in vain.

The post-election victory continued for several weeks, but I had one special day marked on my calendar. It was December 12, 2018, a day I would never forget. It was my official swearing-in ceremony as Deputy Mayor for the Town of Shelburne. My historic achievement would now be made official, surrounded by members of Council, family, and some of my closest friends. When I took the oath of public office that evening, I remember seeing the smiles and obvious pride on the faces of my family, particularly those of my children. After all, this was for them as much as it was for me. They stuck with me through the highs and lows, so it was only fitting that they would be involved in a moment that would be celebrated for years to come.

With my closest supporters firmly behind me, it was now time to validate the community's choice of Deputy Mayor. With the celebration officially over, I was ready to step onto the biggest stage of my life with my vision to make "Shelburne Stronger Together."

Chapter 10

Shelburne Stronger Together—The Birth of a Movement!

"When we all help each other out, when we stand together, we are
stronger together."
– Hillary Clinton

M Y MESSAGE OF a stronger, livable, and prosperous community for all was captured in my campaign slogan, "Shelburne Stronger Together." It was not just about economic prosperity; it was about each person truly caring for, and genuinely looking out for, one another. The slogan was intended to capture the essence of our community and inspire generations to follow. True success would be achieved with the community pulling together in the same direction. My sincere desire was to help shape a community where every person, regardless of race, religion, or gender, felt acknowledged, celebrated, and included in the forward progress of the community. While it appeared that I was striving for a form of utopia, I firmly believed in my heart that such a community was possible. "Shelburne Stronger Together" was not just another campaign slogan; it was meant to be a lifestyle. To have the desired impact, I would have to lead by example.

The idea for the slogan was born after brainstorming with my childhood friend Andrew E. Guy. I specifically chose him for this task because he possessed the unique ability to tap into your soul and get the best out of you. I knew better not to surround myself with individuals who were just quick to rubber stamp anything I had to say without significant input. I could count on Andrew to tell me exactly what I needed to hear, whether I liked it or not.

During the process, he strongly discouraged coming up with flashy and empty lines void of substance. He would often say, "You are not a typical politician; you have been called at this time for something greater." His ability to see far beyond what I could in the moment forced me to tap into something that was authentic, meaningful, and honest. I reflected on my own journey growing up in the Jane and Finch community and the factors that led to my current success. It dawned on me that the recurring theme was how people, at different stages of my life, had worked to support, inspire, encourage, and shape my drive to succeed. This approach worked for me, so why wouldn't it work for the community at large?

Like magic, the slogan appeared: "Shelburne Stronger Together." I smiled and pumped my fists several times, careful not to knock anything over in the room. I was elated that after days of hard work, and a lot of crumpled paper, we were able to come up with something meaningful that spoke to me as a person. Andrew, never one to get too carried away in the moment, stood up from the table and firmly said, "Steve, people are going to judge you by this. Don't use it if you're not prepared to live it." I admired Andrew for his truth serum, but I was prepared more than ever. I knew what a community of supporters had done to enrich my life, and I was determined to do the same for others. A community where each person feels supported is one that becomes a desirable place to live.

My first course of action following the selection of my slogan was to create a campaign team that reflected the growing diversity in our town. It was important right from the start to show how people from various backgrounds can come together and work successfully towards a common goal. My team often joked that we were the United Colours of Benetton. For those too young to remember, during the mid-90s this Italian clothing brand was arguably one of the world's most recognizable fashion brands, using culturally diverse models to sell very colourful pieces. For many people, this company symbolized the importance of diversity and inclusion, and how that can translate to success on a global stage.

With the hard work of everyone involved, I was able to win the election. The victory gave new life and meaning to the slogan. It was clear that the community believed in what I and my team stood for. Our success was proof that diversity is our strength and evidence of what we can achieve when we put aside our perceived differences and work together. Almost immediately, the media and the community began using the slogan. It was surreal to see the support come so quickly.

With the Town of Shelburne growing rapidly and increasingly becoming more diverse, my election victory and vision for our community came at the right time. Such growth over a short period of time can tear many communities apart, especially in a small town where the differences are much more noticeable and people have a hard time accepting change. Andrew was right. I was not here to be another standard politician. I was determined to have Shelburne seen as a model of embracing growth and diversity.

In the distant past, Shelburne had captured national attention for its Fiddle Park Parade, especially the Fiddle Championship. The event drew entertainers, media, and people from across the world, all de-

Figure 10.1: Celebrating with members of our diverse community

scending on our small town. While that status and attention had long faded, it was time to reintroduce Shelburne as one of the most desirable communities to live and initiate commercial investments. I often say that I moved to Shelburne in search of affordable housing but stayed because of the people.

To continue the early momentum of my election victory, it was important to reach out to our community organizations, businesses, media, and faith-based groups to join me in putting into practice our shared vision for the town.

The better the collaboration, the greater the success. The secret ingredient to effective change is to have everyone participate in the evolution of the community. Since my swearing in as Deputy Mayor, some of my proudest moments have come from hearing residents, new and old, beaming about the increased community pride. The source of the pride was not developed by accident, but through intentional work. Following my appointment to Council in 2017, I worked extremely hard on initiatives designed to bring our growing community together. With many other initiatives led by Council and community-based organizations, Shelburne continues to capture the attention of families across Canada. I have been blessed to receive numerous messages from homebuyers thirty-five minutes away in Brampton to as far as Saskatchewan who are interested in moving to our town because of the values we represent. I firmly believe that a community is not considered great because of its smooth roads and shiny sewer pipes, although important. Rather, a community is great when people feel that they belong and are appreciated.

What started off as a slogan created with the help of a friend has become a rallying call for community pride and unity. This incredible journey allowed me to take a deep dive into myself, assessing my God-given gifts and political purpose. I did not want to represent the status quo or simply repeat the usual political promises. I was determined to be a disrupter of normalcy for positive change. Being celebrated for lowering taxes and creating jobs is good, but my goal is to be remembered for my ability to inspire and bring people together. Based on the early feedback, I am doing just that.

Finding Your Calling Is the Best Gift to Yourself and Everyone Around You

On your personal journey, it is often difficult to find out what makes you tick and what your true calling is in life. Unfortunately, many people go through life never making that magical connection. Mark Twain once said, "The two most important days in your life are the day you are born, and the day you find out why." A few years before getting into politics, I was at a book-signing event at Chapters-Indigo in Oakville for my friend Andrew, who was promoting his new book, *Work Your Words*, a self-help book designed to help you discover your true purpose. He was about to start his presentation when a gentleman approached him and said that he had picked up the book and skimmed through the first few pages. He proceeded to say that he was in his mid-sixties and had yet to discover his true purpose in life. Andrew said a few encouraging words, signed his book, and the man left, seemingly determined to change the trajectory of his life. That moment stuck with me long after we had departed. It forced me to analyze my own life and path. How many of us feel the same way this gentleman did? How many of us go through life never discovering our true purpose? That day, I promised not to let my life pass by without finding my purpose and achieving true fulfillment.

Finding out what I was meant to do did not happen overnight. It took me many years to discover my true purpose. I thought that after being told that I would be a good lawyer by my Grade 11 law teacher, I had discovered my path. Fast-forward, I was working as a successful lawyer for one of the largest transit companies in the world. I had made it—I was making good money and living a good lifestyle. However, making good money and living your purpose is not necessarily the same. It is not uncommon to hear of those who are financially stable but still unfulfilled.

A few years into the job as a lawyer, that person was me. Something was missing. I felt and knew that I needed to do more. That is when I discovered a path that was never once on my radar: politics. Immediately, I knew this was where I needed to be. The magic moment finally happened. I had found my purpose. Here I felt most optimal and authentic, and it was where I could use my talents to positively impact the lives of people in my community and beyond. I would never be compensated in the same way as a lawyer, but I did not care. This work brought me the satisfaction I was missing.

True happiness is not about how much money you can make or how famous you can be; it is about living the life you were meant to live. It is about using your talents to bless others.

Chapter 11

It Is Important to Give After You Have Received

"I have shown you in all things that by working hard in this way we must help the weak, remembering the words that the Lord himself said, there is more happiness in giving than in receiving."
– King James Bible: *Acts 20:35.*

S UCCESS IS THE result of hard work, learning from your mistakes, and persistence. It is often said that there is no better feeling than when you set a goal and achieve it. Although I would agree that personal success is rewarding, in my view there is no better feeling than giving someone else a helping hand to achieve their goals. A quote from Harriett Jackson Brown Jr. sums up this mindset: "Remember that the happiest people are not those getting more, but those giving more." I was fortunate growing up to have individuals who took the time to counsel and guide me towards success. There was no hidden agenda or strings attached. They invested in me because they saw potential. It was understood that when I reached my goals, I would pay it forward by investing my time with someone else.

Developing the Attitude of Service—Promising to Give and Deliver

"People with good intentions make promises.
People with good character keep them."
–Unknown

A commitment to service is not a trait you are born with. It is a value system developed over time, often starting with a key moment or turning point in your life. My commitment to give back started long before attaining the highly coveted position at the TTC and before being elected Deputy Mayor for the Town of Shelburne. It was the traumatic separation of my parents that set everything into motion. It was then that I made the promise to my mother that I would take care of her. Finishing school and starting my career could not come fast enough. I was eager to provide her with the opportunities and experiences she could only dream of as a single mother caring for eight children.

My words at the time did not have the same backing as they do today. However, they were made earnestly as an acknowledgement of my mother's sacrifice. It was not until I had graduated from law school at the University of Ottawa and landed a job with the Toronto Transit Commission that I could start to fulfill the promises I had made to her years ago. My salary afforded me the opportunity to expose her to a lifestyle she deserved. We had dinners at some of the most prestigious restaurants in Toronto, attended world-class stage productions, and travelled the world with my two children. I was happiest during these moments, just seeing the smile of gratitude light up her face. As much as my mother appreciated the material show of affection, it was the quality time spent that mattered the most.

Now much older, my mother and I are comfortable having conversations that were previously off the table as a youth growing up in a Caribbean household. As a child, you were never allowed to participate in adult conversations, much less question an adult about their life. Because of this cultural barrier, for many years I did not know much about my mother's background, dreams, and ambitions. It took a cruise in 2015 for our relationship to evolve. It was our first time taking a trip without my children being present. We did everything together, including having in-depth conversations. It was then that I learned about her favourite colour, how she met my father, and her dreams of becoming a dressmaker as a child. Having the opportunity to learn more about her outside of her role as caregiver certainly enriched our relationship. Over the years, I have received so much from my mother, but the greatest gift was getting to know her as a person. No amount of spending on my mother will ever equate to what she has done, and continues to do, for me, but I am committed to continuing her legacy and making her proud for the rest of our lives.

Giving Must First Start at Home

"Your children are great imitators.
So, give them something great to imitate."
–Unknown

With my success as a TTC lawyer and my recent achievement of becoming the Deputy Mayor of the Town of Shelburne, I was eager to make my presence felt in the community. However, before stepping outside to tackle the world, my first order of business was to start at home with my own two children. With my accumulated knowledge, it was important to pass on an honest assessment of the lessons learned and emphasize what was possible if they worked hard and pushed beyond their fears and doubts. Oftentimes, we ask our children to do things we ourselves have not done or are not prepared to do. I was determined along my journey to be an example of what was possible. I would frequently say to my children, "Nothing is off limits if you believe." If I was going to ask them to get comfortable with being un-comfortable, I had to lead the way. I had to overcome my own fears and reservations.

My encouragement was not void of the realities that Black and other racialized children face in their pursuit of success. It is impossible to ignore the inequalities and systemic barriers designed to undermine those efforts. However, it was necessary to impart a message of hope and optimism. My rise from humble beginnings to making history—becoming the first Black lawyer at the Toronto Transit Commission and Deputy Mayor of the Town of Shelburne—was all I needed to prove that despite life's challenges, success is still attainable at the highest level. With my children fully equipped, focused, and confident about their own pursuits, I was ready to take my message of hope and inspiration to the wider community.

Going Back to Where It All Started

Always remember your roots.
They are the foundation of your life and the wings of your future.
– Unknown

Even though my roots were now firmly established in the Town of Shelburne, it was important that I continue my involvement in the community where my journey began. Alongside my best friend, Ian, a lawyer, we came up with the Anderson & Daley Achievement Awards, designed to recognize student excellence in academics, sports, and community service. The objective was clear: we wanted to celebrate student achievement, while motivating others to reach similar heights. An inspired generation is a generation that succeeds. Both Ian and I understood the magnitude of our presence with the youths we were interacting with. We were also fully aware of the importance of lever-aging our professional connections to create educational experiences

Figure 11.1: One of the many graduation ceremonies that Ian and I attended

often not available in marginalized communities. Wanting to show the students our long-term commitment to them, we were regulars during Black History Month events, Career Day workshops, awards assemblies, and year-end graduation ceremonies.

As an elected politician, I was proud to introduce the students to our political system and provincial leaders with organized trips to Queen's Park. For many of them, this was their first time interacting with their local political representatives. Ian and I were routinely told by parents and school officials that the students were responding well to our presence and message of hope. I firmly believe that our strong connection with these youths was largely due to our authenticity and experiences, having grown up in the area. We were not outsiders who did not understand the issues and struggles. Regardless of our achievements, it was important for us to remain within reach and not appear too high in status that students felt disconnected from us. Being humble and approachable was something we both took great pride in.

Having attended many school functions over the years, Ian and I were always moved to hear a young girl or boy say to us, "When I grow up, I want to be like you." Without hesitation, we would both say, "Don't be like us, strive to be better." The mentorship work and time commitments were difficult at times, but we were always refuelled by the genuine feedback received from students across the events we were honoured to participate in. The following are direct quotes from some of the students at Shoreham Public Sports and Wellness Academy located in the Jane and Finch community.

"I learned that we should treat people equally and fairly. We should stand up for ourselves if someone tries to bully us."

"I am almost ten years old. My favourite thing to do is play basketball. Black History is about how we should not hate each other. We should be a team and appreciate diversity. I thank you for being a good leader."

"I am 10 years old. I learned that African Heritage Month is about equality. We all need to be respected because we all have rights. I promise to respect everyone."

"Thank you for coming each year for our graduation. Thank you for even coming."

"Thank you for coming to our school and inspiring us to work hard."

"I can't wait until you come to our school again so I can learn more about you."

Although Ian and I appreciate the accolades, we have benefited from the working partnership with some of the community's best educators, namely Speech-Language Pathologist Tony Wray, Elementary Teacher Rula Ibrahim, Principal Harpreet Ghuman, Principal Boris Stoikos, Vice-Principal Nicole Ferguson-Walker, and many more who consistently go above the call of duty to motivate, inspire, encourage, and prepare our students for the future.

Providing meaningful educational experiences for our students requires planning and collaboration. Ian and I are delighted to be part

Figure 11.2: Ian and I being recognized by the staff and students at Brookview Middle School

of a team committed to investing in our youths. What started off with two men from the Jane and Finch community wanting to give back and make a difference has evolved to include the participation of other professionals and corporate partners, such as the Jane and Finch Mall. Ten years later, we continue to be present, to show what is possible.

Anderson Family Leaving a Legacy of Giving

> *"Giving back to the communities and institutions that helped us achieve success is a value we share and a privilege we embrace."*
> – Dinesh Paliwal

Among all the awards created and distributed, one of my proudest moments came when I was able to share the stage with my mother at an awards ceremony in the Jane and Finch community. I had asked her to accompany me one evening on the premise of showing her the wonderful students Ian and I have been working with. Unknown to her, I had created an award in her name called the "Carmen Anderson Perseverance Award." My plan was to call my mother on stage to help me give it to a deserving student. The gesture was intended to honour her sacrifice and ability to overcome in the face of hardships. It was a public acknowledgement of the qualities that inspired my own journey. The award would be given to a student who demonstrated the ability to thrive despite encountering adversity. When I called her to the stage and began to introduce her, I only got through the first few words before becoming overwhelmed with emotion. Attempting to speak about the inspiration behind the award had me remembering how my mother consistently put her family before herself without any complaints.

I was fully aware that the graduation was not about us, but for a moment I wanted to celebrate my mother. When I finally finished her introduction, she took the stage and directed her comments to the parents and guardians in the audience. Her encouraging words and lessons learned really resonated with everyone. To my surprise, she received a standing ovation, leaving hardly a dry eye in the room. The moment was beyond what I had expected and was one we would cherish for the rest of our lives. The award in my mother's name firmly established her legacy and influence over the younger generation.

Aside from my mother, one of my biggest heroes continues to be my older brother Clive. As I shared in my story, he was a respected basketball player and academic stand-out in the Jane and Finch community who inspired many, including me, to take up the sport. For much of my high school experience, I was eager to show Clive that I belonged on the same sporting stage as him. Although I was unable to capture the same level of success, years later I would get more than I ever could imagine. As highly respected lawyers, Clive and I would stand shoulder

A PLACE CALLED HOME

Brothers *Clive and Steve Anderson* are products of their environment — and that's a good thing

BY M. BOATENG

n the Toronto Transit Commission's (TTC) corporate board-room, two lawyers are preparing to speak about the neigh-bourhood that facilitated their professional and social suc-cess. Steve Anderson, a top lawyer with the TTC, and older brother, Clive, an internationally-respected legal mind preparing for an upcoming post in Singapore, exude the type of confidence it seems developed by way of private schools, dinner parties of a privileged youth. The two, however, are products of one of Toronto's most maligned "at-risk" areas. "We grew up at Jane and Keystone, right near the Jane and Finch Mall," says Steve. Adds Clive, "People have these ideas about the type of individuals who come out of these areas. The truth is, these neighbourhoods are filled with good people who have a lot to offer."

While many mainstream media outlets portray Jane and Finch areas rife with poverty, violence and crime, the Andersons paint a different picture. Theirs is a portrait framed in the reality of actually having lived in the community. The brothers grew up with a mother who gave education priority one; she required her sons to maintain a certain grade average or have extracurricular activities taken away. "People have...

Steve Anderson (L) and brother Clive

Figure 11.3: Clive and I pictured in the Sway Magazine

to shoulder, representing the Jane and Finch community.

In 2011, Clive and I were honoured to be featured in *Sway Magazine* with the title, "A Place Called Home. Brothers Clive and Steve Anderson are products of the Jane and Finch environment—and that's a good thing." In the article, we paid tribute to our mother and shared our respective journeys to accomplishing success. We stood as examples of the success stories often overlooked in the Jane and Finch community. With our platform, it was necessary to rebut the biases and prejudices that saddle the community.

The feedback from the community was instant, further solidifying our status as role models. Two powerful Black men and brothers from Jane and Finch gave a positive image that the world needed to see. Even if for a moment, our story was a welcome change from the persistent narrative of guns, gangs, drugs, and violence.

Clive and I were proud of our roots and how the community shaped us as individuals. No matter how far we climbed up the ladder, we would never turn our backs on a community that gave us so much. As they said in the neighbourhood, we were "Finch men" for life. While the feature of our story in *Sway Magazine* was satisfying, we knew it was never just not about us. It was an opportunity to ensure that other members of our community would have similar opportunities and successes. We both dedicated our time and resources to ensure just that.

Representation Matters

"Representation is vital otherwise the butterfly surrounded by a group
of moths unable to see itself will keep trying to become the moth."
–Rupi Kaur

Whether in the Jane and Finch community, the Town of Shelburne, or in any other community, the ability to see yourself in potential opportunities is critical to one's belief of what is possible. This is true at any age, but particularly so when you are young and trying to find your path in life. To be honest, I never imagined how far-reaching my election victory would be, and the many lives impacted. After all, I was just the Deputy Mayor of the Town of Shelburne and not the Prime Minister of Canada. I would soon find that the community in Shelburne and beyond felt much differently.

I remember that my first few public appearances were in schools in Shelburne to support community-based initiatives. Every time I was introduced to the student body, I saw widened eyes and dropped mouths once the children realized that their Deputy Mayor was a Black man. The shock was apparent, but so was the sense of pride—not just for Black students but for other racialized groups as well. What the children saw in me were possibilities, and that made me proud. My presence was equally as beneficial for our Caucasian students, since it allowed them to see what other groups were capable of outside of the stereotypical boxes.

One unexpected encounter with a young child reinforced the meaning of my presence in the community. One afternoon, I attended Glenbrook Elementary School in Shelburne to provide a certificate to the Grade 8 championship basketball team. After presenting the certificate and taking photos, I was preparing to leave, when I noticed a little Black girl standing near the entrance of the gymnasium, holding the hand of her teacher. She was staring in my direction, but I thought nothing of it at the time. I smiled at her and turned my back, ready to leave, when the teacher called my name and asked to have a moment of my time. With the young girl in hand, she said that the student had patiently waited to say hello to me. I crouched down to greet her, and she said, "I know you and so do my parents. I am so happy to see you."

I said, "Thank you, I am happy to see you as well. Please tell your parents I said hello."

Following a warm embrace, we both had the biggest smiles on our faces before she ran off and disappeared into the gymnasium. At first blush, it was a simple and brief interaction, but the mere fact she felt comfortable approaching someone in a position of authority that looked like her was a big moment for the both of us. I left that experience, promising to never take for granted my presence and the impact it had on people.

Although it was still early in my political career, I would like to share a few quotes that demonstrate how my election to a position of authority has impacted those in Shelburne and beyond.

"Hey Steve, was thinking about you today and the example that you are setting for future generations. Admire the work you are doing. I think you would make an awesome Prime Minister, would love to see you be the first. Keep up the great work."

"I have seen the work you are doing in the community, and I couldn't resist feeling so proud. Congratulations!"

"I am encouraged by your position as Deputy Mayor of Shelburne. Keep

fighting the good fight and making strides. God Bless."

"I decided to request to be added to your network because it was such a desire to see a Black man in your role. I do believe that representation matters and I'm happy that my son will be able to see someone like you in this role."

"I was very impressed with your accomplishments, many of which I am trying to achieve for myself. I was wondering if you have any advice or suggestions for me."

"Hi Steve, Hope you are doing well. Since we connected on LinkedIn last month, I have been keeping up with your posts and continue to be inspired by the great work you are doing in the community. I am writing to see if it is possible for us to have a call in the next few weeks whenever your schedule permits so we can get to know each other and start a mentor-mentee relationship."

These statements are just another reminder of the significance of my platform and the responsibilities that come along with it. Yes, I am the Deputy Mayor for the entire Shelburne community, but I cannot ignore the significance of my presence and how it can be used to inspire and motivate Black and other racialized persons to achieve success. I am honoured to be an example of what is possible when we are determined not to let anyone hold us back.

Striking the Right Balance

The desire to give back to your community does not come without personal sacrifice. With my growing popularity came increased demands on my time. In the beginning, it was difficult to balance my desire to give back and the numerous requests for public appearances. Knowing how much my presence, words, or actions could potentially change the trajectory of someone's life, I wanted to say yes to every invitation, and I did. Unfortunately, I learned the hard way that this approach would not be sustainable in the long run. I needed to find a different strategy to avoid flaming out too quickly. It was important to replenish myself, so I was not depleted when people needed me the most.

In essence, I had to learn to say no on occasions, despite how difficult it was. Whether it is the giving of a material gift or yourself, it should always come from a place of sincerity, joy, and the desire to see other people happy. If your desire to help starts to make you unhappy, it is time to step back and re-evaluate. Before you can give to anyone else, you must first give the requisite attention to yourself.

I have learned many lessons from experienced politicians and other public servants who have contributed to my learning curve and success as Deputy Mayor. However, the most important lessons came from my mother. It was her leadership and guidance from the very beginning that shaped me into the man I have become today.

Chapter 12

Lessons Learned from My Mother

T HE SONG BY legendary rapper Tupac Shakur titled "Dear Mama" appropriately plays in the background as I steer through my thoughts and emotions in preparation for this chapter of the book. There are not enough words to express the value of a mother. She is the foundation of a family and the person who knows how to make you smile when that is the last thing you want to do. She is the one who will sacrifice every aspect of her life to ensure that her children and family have a better life. Her every action, step, and movement are not for herself but for others, and she does not seek any praise, attention, or recognition for her efforts.

Author Rachel Martin sums it up best: "A mother is emotional, yet the rock. Tired, but keeps going. Worried, but full of hope. Impatient, yet patient. Overwhelmed, but never quits. Amazing, even though doubted. Wonderful, even in the chaos. Life changer, every single day." While writing this book, I reflected on the lessons learned from my mother and how they are still relevant today. Thinking about the many teaching moments, it would be impossible to capture everything

Figure 12.1: My mother in her early 20's

in a single chapter. After much thought, I picked four short stories that reflect the essence of her character. Although my mother's influence on me is mentioned throughout this book, this final chapter was written to honour her ongoing legacy.

Story #1: Work Ethic—My Mother's Mamba Mentality

Social media and the internet are filled with legendary stories of hard-working individuals and their work ethic. The stories of Michael Jordan, Kobe Bryant, Lebron James, Barak Obama, and Bill Gates are examples of those who fit the criteria. They serve as a source of inspiration, especially when we struggle to find it within our circle of family and friends.

In my life, I was fortunate to have a mother who gave me all the inspiration I needed, demonstrating a work ethic that would rival any superstar athlete. As a youth, I recall being startled from my sleep, hearing my mother getting ready every morning at 5:00 AM to be out the door by 6:00 AM. When the rest of the family woke up, we would always find breakfast prepared and left on the table. Considering the little amount of time she had to get ready, we were always astonished to see her outward display of love before she disappeared for work.

My mother's work was not glamorous or well paying; she grinded out a living as a machine operator in a paper factory. Regardless of the weather, she was determined to get to work, always cognizant of the fact that she was a single mother with eight children to take care of. In over twenty-five years at the McDermid Paper Factory, my mother was never late nor did she ever use the allotted vacation time on herself. Instead, at the end of the year she would opt for a cash pay-out for the unused vacation days. My mother understood that our family would benefit from every dollar in hand. A leisurely trip to enjoy the warm Caribbean sun was not meant to be. Her commitment to her work and our family left a positive impact on us all. Earning just over $30,000 a year would not impact her quality of work. Her reputation as a dedicated and honest worker earned her tremendous respect among the management team and her coworkers.

I knew of my mother's value in the home, but it was another thing to witness it firsthand at her workplace. In the summer before my last year of high school, I was looking for another job after terminating my employment with United Parcel Service (UPS). This was a difficult decision, because this was my first real job after being fired from my paper route at the age of twelve. I enjoyed my time at UPS, especially working with my best friend Ian. However, the heavy lifting requirements was beginning to take a physical toll. After speaking to Mother about my job searches, she encouraged me to fill out an application at her workplace.

Although hesitant at first, I did, and in a matter of days I was employed. I am certain that my mother's reputation at work played a significant role in my hiring. Truthfully, I was curious as to how things happened so quickly, but I dared not to ask. It was an opportunity to earn some much-needed cash and to witness firsthand what my mother did for a living. Prior to this, I had never seen how my mother performed at work. What she did during her eight-hour shift was left to what she said about her job and my imagination. That summer, I spent months observing her dedication to her craft as a machine operator and how she would often take the time to train, mentor, and encourage her colleagues to be better.

Her selflessness and team-building attitude did not go unnoticed, as she was frequently celebrated as a model employee. Management would often bring new clients to her workstation to demonstrate the production process. This was a great source of pride for her, and I was honoured to witness it all. The indelible lesson was clear: Work hard and take pride in everything you do. Whether at school, church, work, or with friends, the way you carry yourself adds or subtracts from your reputation each day. Like my mother, your positive reputation can open doors for you and others around you. From that summer on, my work ethic, and how I decided to carry myself, took on a new meaning.

Story #2: Never Make Excuses, No Matter How Difficult Things Become

During my childhood, my father decided to leave our household without warning, suddenly turning our lives upside down. We were all unsettled with the sudden turn of events. I vowed never to muster a positive word about him, considering what he had done to us. During this tumultuous period, it would have been understandable, if not expected, that my mother would display bouts of anger against my father or have periodic rants, blaming him for our current predicament. If it occurred, I would have happily added my voice to the chorus of complaints. To my surprise, she never once complained about my father or the unwelcomed circumstances she now faced. My mother was determined to soldier on as if nothing had changed. At times, I was left to wonder whether she was in complete denial of our situation. We were all hurting in one way or the other, so I was mesmerized by her ability to put emotions aside for the sake of providing normalcy for the household. It was her determination, attitude, and steadiness in the face of hardship that gave us the confidence that everything would be okay. The bills were paid on time, groceries were purchased, and love was constantly permeating throughout the household.

As I reflect on that period of my life, I can only begin to imagine the level of strength and fortitude it took to conceal her emotions, fears, and doubts during it all, appearing unfazed by the unknown that surrounded her. Knowing my mother, the answer is to be found in her deep faith in God, trusting that in difficult times, He always provides. It was her resolve and spiritual beliefs that made me adopt the mantra "No excuses" when facing my own challenges. Obstacles, setbacks, and disappointments are par for the course in the journey called life. It is how you respond to these situations that defines who you are and your character. I am reminded of the quote by Stephen Covey that says, "We develop our character muscles by overcoming challenges and obstacles." I was determined never to allow real or perceived obstacles to prevent me from fulfilling my dreams. As the saying goes, when life gives you lemons, make lemonade.

Story #3: Investing in Others

My mother's commitment to putting her children's needs over her own was on full display throughout my childhood. However, one example consistently brings tears of appreciation to my eyes whenever I recall the moment.

It was during my second year at the University of Windsor when I received a phone call from my mother. I could immediately tell by her voice that something was wrong. She tried to speak, but I had difficulty understanding through the tears and heavy breathing. After calming her down, she confided in me that she had been recently laid off from her job. My mother was devastated, and why wouldn't she be? She had been a valued employee for over twenty-five years. In a state of shock, I wondered how this was possible.

I was desperate to find the words to console her, but it felt as if my lips were sealed with glue. I finally said, "Mom, it's probably best that you finally have a period of rest and the opportunity to pursue some of your own interests." She paused for a few seconds and said, "Steve, I just wanted to work long enough to ensure that you got off to a good start financially." I was stunned when I heard those words. A mixed feeling of pain and gratitude shot throughout my body. After getting off the phone, I went home and sobbed for hours. This was yet again another example of her sacrifice. The magnitude of the moment was overwhelming. I was certain that something had to be done. My mother had always been there when I needed her the most; it was time to return the favour, even though I was hours away in another city.

Without telling her, I purchased a Greyhound bus ticket that would have me arrive in Toronto early the next morning. Upon my arrival, I headed directly to her workplace in Mississauga. Thinking back, I should have contacted her former employer about my desire to visit, but at that point there was no turning back. I was determined to be heard. I had no clue what I would accomplish by speaking to the owner, but I needed answers. With my presence unexpected, I was pleasantly surprised when the owner agreed to meet with me in the lobby. I was there for a purpose, so when he finally came outside, I immediately got to my first question, "How could you do this to my mother?" He spoke sincerely about my mother and the twenty-five years of service given to his company. He repeated that the decision was extremely difficult, but the company was downsizing, and he had no choice. After a lengthy discussion, I calmed down, taking the time to make sense of his decision. I could not change the outcome, but I left the meeting proud of her reputation, legacy, and sacrifice at the company. I relayed the conversation to my mother, who was disappointed with the outcome but appreciative of my actions and the kind words from her now former boss.

My mother's layoff story is unfortunately very familiar for many families across Canada. However, it was her commitment to my personal development that made me feel unique and special. I would later apply her sacrificial spirit when raising my own two children. Like many parents, I would do anything, within reason, to assist my children in meeting their full potential. Along my journey towards success, I benefited directly from those who had invested their time and resources to allow me to become the person I am today. Now financially secure, it gives me great joy to pay it forward, ensuring many others have the same opportunity to achieve success.

Story #4: Anything Is Possible When You Have Faith

We now live in a time when any profession of faith or belief in God is seen as strange, obsolete, or out-of-touch with current societal standards. Tik Tok, Google, YouTube, and Netflix have become the popular choices for millions seeking inspiration and guidance. When I think about my mother, the greatest gift she has given our family is her unwavering faith in God as a source of strength. Every weekend during my childhood, my mother would gather the family and haul us on public transportation to attend church services. At the beginning, I struggled to understand her willingness to sacrifice precious weekend time just to attend church over an hour away from home. In my mind, I imagined our family doing things that were more entertaining, such as watching movies, visiting friends, or going to the park. Instead, we would spend the entire day among other devoted families, listening to the pastor emphasize the importance of having faith during the peaks and valleys of one's life. That message would often be followed by the hymn, "A Shelter in the Time of Storm."

For my mother, going to church was just as important as going to work. It was here that she would cultivate her faith to help withstand life's inevitable challenges. From day one, my mother had a master plan. It was her desire that we, too, would connect to the same source in our time of need. To be clear, having faith does not shelter you from the challenges and disappointments life has to offer, but it provides hope that things will get better if you persevere. Considering what my mother had to endure following the separation from my father, it was clear that her faith was what saw her through. Having my own belief system would prove to be crucial. Simply put, without cultivating my own faith, I could not imagine overcoming my own struggles that appeared insurmountable at the different stages in my life. With each new challenge, I was confident that God would help me overcome. Having now read my story, you are likely to agree that I received assistance from a higher power. Whether or not you attend a religious institution or believe in God, the point remains the same: One must have hope, no matter how difficult things get. Oftentimes, life does not go as planned, but we must stay the course, always striving to be our best selves.

Figure 12.2: My mom and I outside her home in Brampton

Chapter 13

Conclusion

I wrote this book as a leap of faith, not knowing exactly how revisiting my childhood would make me feel. It is never easy to resurrect the memories and emotions you have spent your lifetime trying to keep buried. Despite my initial trepidation, I am glad to have garnered the strength to complete this journey. With honour, pride, and gratitude, I dedicate this book to my family, friends, supporters, and to the two communities that have given me so much—Jane and Finch and the Town of Shelburne.

To all the parents, mentors, teachers, and organizations who have played an instrumental role in the development of our youth, and continue to do so today, this book is a salute to you as well. My story firmly establishes that we all can achieve great things, regardless of race, religion, gender, or sexual orientation, if we collectively take the time to support each other. Let us not allow bias, prejudice, and stereotypes to prevent us from lending a helping hand to someone who needs our kindness the most.

Finally, to all youths, continue to dream big, regardless of your current situation. If things are difficult, let me reassure you that, in time, life will get better. Continue to put in the work, have faith, and surround yourself with people who will help you achieve your goals. Remember, success for most of us does not happen overnight. It may sound unpopular but be patient and remain focused until your turn comes. In essence, stay in your lane and try not to focus on how fast other people are moving around you. When you reach the end of your journey, make it a point to honour and celebrate those who have helped you along the way.

Lastly, pay it forward by using your platform to help others who are just as hungry to achieve their goals. Always remember, we are Stronger Together!

Manufactured by Amazon.ca
Bolton, ON

23120844R00109